**CRETAN COOKING**
*The miracle of the Cretan Diet*
*The most wholesome cuisine*
*in the Mediterranean*

**NEW REVISED EDITION 2000**

Translation of the new, revised edition:
**Maria Bitsakaki**
**Melanie Goodwin**

Photography: **Nikos Psilakis**

Lay-out: **Nikos Dretakis**

Printing: **TYPOKRETA**

ISBN: 960-7448-24-3

MARIA & NIKOS PSILAKIS

# Cretan Cooking

*The miracle of the Cretan diet*
*The most wholesome cuisine in the Mediterranean*

With **265** Recipes

KARMANOR

# C O N T

# E N T S

# RECIPES

# FOREWORD

On an international scale, there's much discussion in the scientific community about, and deep interest in, finding the ideal diet which will improve the health of people. Ever since antiquity, the traditional diet of the Cretans seems to be just such a one, including all the right ingredients. A comparative study among several developed countries, which began in 1960 on behalf of seven countries, has a group of about 700 Cretan men from the rural areas under medical observation, regularly checking the state of their health. So far this group has had the lowest percentage of deaths caused by heart attacks and different kinds of cancer. This study has also shown the Cretan population to be the longest living one. When, in 1991, thirty one years after the beginning of the study, the Social Health Sector of the University of Crete undertook the medical check-up of the members of the group, about 50% were found to be still alive as opposed to Finland where there wasn't a single survivor!

Cretans have been able to enjoy such perfect health and long life thanks to their diet. Until recently this diet was simple and wholesome: olive oil of course, which accounted for one third of the individual's daily energy needs, but mainly cereals, principally bread, pulses, vegetables and fruit and, to a lesser degree, cheese, milk, eggs, fish and a little red wine with every meal. Unfortunately, this diet has undergone some changes in the last few decades, mainly among the younger generations, with most undesirable results for the general state of health of the population: a noticeable increase in early deaths caused by heart attacks and a widespread increase in malignant neoplasm. For this reason, every effort which aims at restoring the traditional Cretan diet is of great importance.

The editions by KARMANOR, through their valuable efforts to put together traditional recipes from all over the island have acted as pioneers in this new field.

The recipes of traditional Cretan cooking published in this book explain the eating habits of the Cretans and the choices that have guided Cretan cooking up to the last few decades. The first chapter of the book gives a detailed account of the simple and wholesome diet followed by Cretans in the past. Nowadays it is easy to choose from such an amount of recipes those which are best suited to our modern way of life. Up to the beginning of the 1960s Cretan peasants walked an average of 13 kilometres a day and today

70% of the Cretan population walks less than 2 kilometres daily! This is why the modern inhabitants of the island don't need as many calories; therefore rich and fatty food should be eaten very occasionally or even not at all.

Taking the conditions of modern life into account, we would recommend a return to the traditional Cretan eating habits, but with a noticeable decrease in the amount and frequency in the consumption of meat and other animal products. On the other hand, cereals (mainly bread), pulses, vegetables and fruit should represent 85% of our daily food. The consumption of olive oil must be continued; it has been proven through several past and present studies that this excellent oil plays an all-important role in warding off illnesses and in preserving our good health. Contrary to other vegetable oils, olive oil is rich in mo-nounsaturated fatty acids which are resistant to oxidation and diminish the amount of LDL cholesterol without affecting the HDL cholesterol.

This last one is a protection against atherosclerosis, whereas other vegetable oils are rich in polyunsaturated fatty acids and are sensitive to oxidation, producing LDL peroxides and oxides, which are particularly atherogenic.

Moreover, olive oil contains a vast amount of anti-oxidative agents like tokopherols and hydroxyphenols which, by bonding free toxic radicals, are a natural protection against atherosclerosis and different kinds of cancer. It is interesting to note that the composition of olive oil in fatty acids is similar to that of maternal milk.

Cretan traditional cooking makes use exclusively of olive oil, achieving excellent results both in taste and health levels; it is therefore highly advisable not to replace it with any other vegetable oil, for this is not suitable for cooking and frying. This is also the case of different sorts of margarine, a hydrogenation of vegetable oils and olive oil, as this product was completely unknown in traditional Greek cooking until a few decades ago. All these products contain fatty acids which are dangerous for one's health.

The Cretan recipes in this book, which have been arduously put together by the authors, give younger generations judicious advice and the opportunity to live on a perfect diet, avoiding the diets that derive from oriental religions, which often have drastic and negative effects on one's health. A return to the traditional Cretan eating habits is a way of maintaining one's health and lessening the odds of falling victim to the plague of modern illnesses, such as heart attacks and cancer. Traditional Cretan cooking offers modern man a great food variety both in dishes and tastes, prepared on the basis of pure and natural products.

To conclude, the authors of the book make a specific note of the Cretan diet during the religious fasting periods of the Orthodox Church; indeed this regular vegetarianism, as established by the Orthodox Church, and in no way comparable to the strict and dangerous vegetarianism imposed by some food-faddists, seems to have excellent healthy results and is the object of a special research by the Social Health Sector of the University of Crete.

*Antonis Kafatos*
*Professor of Preventive Medicine*
*and Nutrition, University of Crete*

Natural, traditional and local produce which give a clean taste to the food, combined with the lovely customs of the local population, are the hallmarks of traditional Cretan cooking. The roots of these traditions go way back in time, to those distant times which have bequeathed to the Cretans their love of life and good food.

The complex habits of the modern consumer have supplanted many typical traits of traditional Cretan cooking and the original tastes of the Cretans. The great effort on the part of the authors of this book to group old and forgotten recipes from all over Crete, and to publish them together with some that are still in use nowadays, has filled us with enthusiasm. It is our experience that traditional Cretan cooking appeals as much to the local population as to the foreigners who visit our island, offering them not only one of the most savoury and healthy cuisine in the world, but also introducing them to a unique, century-old civilisation.

The Cretan Association of Hotel Directors strongly recommends this book as a means of implementing the traditional Cretan recipes that figure in it, in hotels all over the island. In this way, local tradition will provide us with precious elements, like the authenticity of tastes, the use of local products and the love and enjoyment of life.

*Kostas Komninos*
*President of the Association*
*of Hotel Directors*

An important gap in the selection, re-cording, documentation and propagation of our gastronomic wealth has now been filled through the inestimable contribution of this new book.

Methodical and with great sensiti-vity, the authors give us a complete picture of the historical development of Cretan cooking from the Minoans, the Deipnosophists and the Byzantines up to the present day, pointing out the cultural unity of the Greek world, and at the same time, emphasizing the specialities of each region.

This long and laborious effort is presented in a simple and understandable way. The book includes introductory notes to each unit of recipes, folkloric background to the various dishes, frequent references to the nutritional and wholesome elements of the Cretan diet (particularly olives, olive-oil, greens and the whole range of herbs). The recipes have been given to the authors by the very people who put them into practice in their every day life. All this, and last, but not least, the rich illustrations, are an important contribution to the effort for preserving and propagating our Cretan gastronomic tradition.

*Nikos Skoulas*
*ex-Minister of Tourism*

*Sheep and goats grazing near the Libyan Sea, at sunset*

# THE MIRACLE OF THE CRETAN DIET

The Cretan diet is today considered to be the ideal human diet: a valuable commodity which ensures good health and long life.

It is not by chance that international research has found Crete to be the best characteristic example of the internationally renowned Mediterranean diet. In the 1950s, the international scientific community discovered the high level of health of the Cretans.

The good health of the inhabitants of the island is a result of their diet.

Today it is generally agreed that the people who lived on this blessed island and ate according to the traditional ways had less chance of dying from heart diseases. In fact, recent statistics from the **World Health Organisation** (1987) show that diseases related to the heart and its connected vessels were **considerably lower on Crete than in other countries**, as is shown in Table 1.

# THE STUDY
# OF THE SEVEN COUNTRIES

T o reach this conclusion, the international scientific community had to carry out research so that the results could shed no doubt on this fact. A study was first carried out by many researchers to generally prove that various illnesses, such as cardiovascular diseases, were possibly connected with diet. An American doctor, Anzel Keys, managed to scientifically substantiate the important role that diet played in the prevention of diseases and in the general good health of people.

*Cretan men sitting at a traditional coffee house in the village of Archanes*

During the course of the study which started in 1956, 12.763 men between the ages of 40 and 59, from seven different countries and 16 sub-groups were studied. These groups of population came from countries and areas which had varying levels of development, as well as different cultures and habits. To be more precise, those under study were:

3 population groups from Italy, 5 from the former Yugoslavia, 2 from Spain, 2 from Finland, 1 from the Netherlands, 1 from USA and 2 from Greece. Of the two groups from

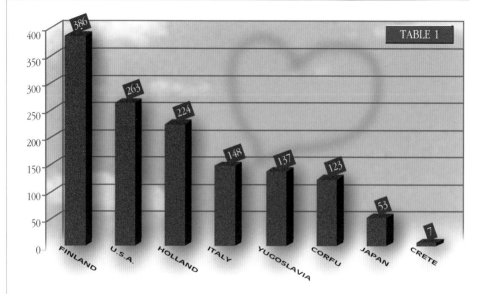

**WORLD HEALTH ORGANIZATION 1987 - CORONARY DEATH RATE PER 100.000**

Greece, one was from Crete and the other was from Corfu. Publication of the first results caused a great deal of discussion. There was one general conclusion, that the inhabitants of the Mediterranean countries experienced better health than those in the northern countries. Most astonishing were the results from Crete where the inhabitants of the island rarely suffered from heart diseases, to such an extent, that it was almost unheard of! Also, the growth of cancer related diseases was decidedly lower in comparison to the other countries in the study.

Table 2 shows the remarkable difference in the death rate due to coronary illnesses between the inhabitants of Crete and the other countries in the Study of Seven Countries and Table 3 records the general death rate of the inhabitants of Crete, according to the same study.

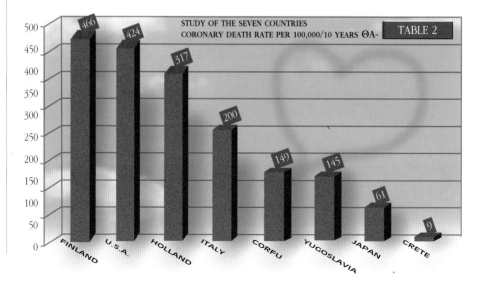

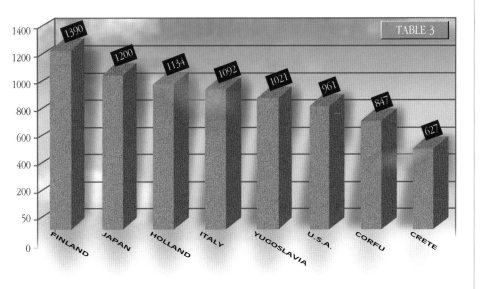

STUDY OF THE SEVEN COUNTRIES - AVERAGE MORTALITY PER 100.000

# SERGE RENAUD'S STUDY

Many years after the study by Anzel Keys, the French professor Serge Renaud thought, quite brilliantly, of using the Cretan dietary prototype as a preventive measure against death in cases where the people had already suffered a heart attack and were under medical observation. These patients were split into two groups. One group ate according to the guidelines set down by the American Cardiological Society, which were, in general, followed by the majority of doctors all over the world. This suggested a low intake of fats. The second group in the study followed the Cretan dietary prototype. Table 3 clearly shows the results. From the group which used the Cretan diet, 8 people died in total whereas from the other group, 20 died. This shows a higher mortality rate of between 70 to 76%.

| TABLE 4 | Number of patients | Cretan Diet | Instructions of the American Cardiological Company | Difference |
|---|---|---|---|---|
| Coronary mortality | 28 | 8 | 20 | 70% |

*Bλ. A. Keys, Seven Countries Study: a multivariate analysis of death and coronary heart disease. Cambridge, Harvard University Press, 1980.
Keys, A. Menotti, C. Aravanis et al. The Seven Countries Study: 2289 deaths in 15 years. Prev Med 1984, 13: 141-154.
Keys, A. Menotti, Mj. Karvonen et al. The diet and 15 year death rate in the Seven Countries Study. Am J Epidemiol 1986, 124: 903-915.
A. Menoti, A. Keys, C. Aravanis et al. Seven Countries Study: first 20 year mortality data in 12 cohorts of six countries. Ann Med 1989, 21: 175 - 179.
C. Aravanis, RP Mensisk, A. Corcondilas et al. Risk factors for coronary heart disease in middle-aged men in Crete in 1982. Int J Epidimiol 1988, 17: 779-783.

# THE CHARACTERISTICS OF THE CRETAN DIET

The high standard of health of the Cretans was a direct result of their diet, or to be more precise, their way of life. In other words, it was the result of diet, exercise, enjoyment of life with company, conversation and wine, which a Cretan never drinks on his own, but in the company of family and friends. This is a deep-rooted Greek custom shared by neighbouring countries where traditions and religious rituals include the consumption of wine.

A Cretan gets nearly all his food from nature. He eats an abundance of fruit and vegetables. The only fat content which he uses in his food and salads is olive oil. Every day, all the family members sit around the table and talk about their daily problems, all enjoying their companionship. Guests are often present. In Greece it is usual to eat in the company of relatives and friends, telling jokes and having fun while enjoying a few glasses of wine which accompany the delicious food.

But what is the difference in the consumption of products between the Cretan diet and the other Greek and Mediterranean areas? The following table shows the characteristics:

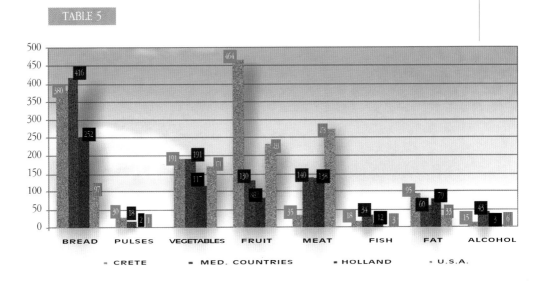

TABLE 5

NUTRITIONAL HABITS PER AREA (grams per day)

■ CRETE   ■ MED. COUNTRIES   ■ HOLLAND   ■ U.S.A.

# The Cretan consumes:

*A Cretan man from the village of Sfakia is cooking the traditional rice pilaff at a feast*

❶ **More fat** (fat substances) than the others, in fact almost three times more than the Americans and one and a half times more than the inhabitants of the Mediterranean areas. Here, there is one main difference, in that the Cretan consumes fat substances but he never or hardly ever eats animal fats or seed oil! To be more specific, he consumes only pure and tasty olive oil! What is more, a substantial amount of the olive oil is eaten without having been boiled or fried, in other words it is used in its raw state on salads or on rusks.

❷ **A small amount of meat**. On Crete, as in other Greek areas, meat was eaten as a part of rituals. Cretans in ancient times ate meat when sacrifices were made. In later times, meat was eaten on days of celebration and only much later, it became a custom whereby meat was eaten every Sunday or every other Sunday.

❸ **Substantial amounts of bread**. Cretans eat three times more bread than the average American but relatively lesser then the amount consumed in the other Mediterranean areas. What should be mentioned is that the Cretan eats or, if we are to be truthful, ate, bread with roughage or as it is called today, **wholemeal flour**. White bread,

*Fishing at a Greek beach*

without roughage, was only eaten on feast days such as at Christmas, Easter and on 15th August. Travellers who visited the island during the Turkish occupation, described the black barley rusks consumed by the inhabitants. The Austrian traveller, F.W. Sieber (1818), tells of the tasty black bread made by the monks of the Holy Trinity of Mourtaros. This was made from wheat, barley and rye.

**❹ A little fish.** Fish was consumed much more in the coastal areas rather than in the hinterland. During periods of fasting, fish, both fresh and salted, was eaten more frequently. Accounts by monks in the Middle Ages and during the Renaissance inform us that the Cretans consumed salted and smoked fish and sea food, but they did not eat this type of food every day. Fish was the basis of their Sunday meals.

**❺ An abundance of fruit!** The Cretans eat more fruit than anybody else, in fact, four times more than the other inhabitants of the Mediterranean, six times more than the Dutch and twice as much as the Americans. Travellers to the island in previous centuries, were amazed by the Cretan fruit, the grapes and the oranges. Nowadays, although technological developments in agriculture have seriously reduced the flavour of farmed products, Cretan fruit is still looked upon very highly. The cultivation of Cretan orchard products, excluding citrus fruits, is not done systematically and so retains the pure, authentic and delicious taste of fruits, such as apricots or peaches. Today, more than ever, anybody can spot the strong and yet aromatic flavour of a pear from the mountain of Dikti or from the parched trees above the village of Krousonas.

❻ **Pulses and vegetables in large amounts.** These are the basis of the daily diet. No more than two or three days would go by without pulses in a meal and not a day would go by without vegetables and local greens! These have become such a staple of every meal that even the lamb eaten at Easter is not consumed on its own. Most Cretans ate lamb with artichokes, lamb with chicory, lamb with lettuce and on some occasions, lamb roasted on the spit. (Spits were used at feasts in the countryside where usual kitchen facilities were not available. The eating of meat out in the country was much closer to the traditions of their ancestors). At Christmas they ate pork with ground wheat, at carnival time meat with dried vegetables, mainly okra or meat with local greens (at this time of year there is an abundance of fennel). In Messara, on the night before a wedding, the official dish was meat with chick peas.

❼ **Wine with their food.** One or, more usually, two glasses of wine. Of course, children were taught this custom at an early age. It is believed that wine is good for you. It seems that they were right! For the Cretan, wine was a complete ritual. People have been seen to spill a few drops of wine on the ground so that "the dead can drink" and not miss out on the joy which is given by the delicious juice of the grape. As has already been mentioned, wine was the binding factor of companionship. A Cretan never drank alone; only with his friends, talking, laughing, enjoying a beautiful sunset and the pure joy of life!

# Uncooked vegetables, olive oil, olives and Cretan rusks

If we try to ascertain the differences in diet between Cretans and the inhabitants of other areas, we will come to the conclusion that the Cretan enjoys authentic tastes. A visitor to the island would be taken aback to see Cretans eating uncooked spine chicory (stamnagathi), which is a wonderful green that grows both on the Cretan mountains and in coastal areas, raw artichokes with a little salt and lemon juice, large amounts of vetchling (the leaves of a leguminous plant which is cultivated on the island) as components of tasty salads. A visitor would also be surprised to see the daily and necessary consumption in the summer of large amounts of purslane with tomato and cucumber. In other Greek areas, this plant is considered to be undesirable, as it is a weed, whereas the Cretans look upon purslane as a blessing. Many countries in the Mediterranean do not even eat purslane! All these uncooked greens are eaten with a large amount of olive oil, the very same one which made such an impression on A. Keys. *"My goodness! They consume so much olive oil!"* This is what he is heard to have said.

On Crete, not a summer's day goes by without notchweed and a little black nightshade, as chicory and, in general, the local greens are a way of life. It is impressive to observe the way in which olive oil is used in the Cretan diet and the traditional cooking of the island. Olive oil on salad, olive oil in food and even olive oil in the traditional sweets! On various occasions, visitors have been unable to believe that the wonderful raisin biscuits which they have been offered were made with olive oil!

Bread and olives are the favourite appetizers of the Cretans. Apart from being full of natural fibrous barley, a rusk is drizzled with olive oil and then covered in finely chopped tomatoes with a sprinkling of salt and oregano on the top, so producing a lovely taste! In Rethymnon, grated white cheese (savoury myzithra) or feta is placed on top of the tomato. A round rusk (kouloura) is used and this is known as "koukouvaja" (owl). This is rarely absent from a professional restaurant which seriously aims to serve traditional food.

The Cretan "stafidolia" (wrinkled olive) is another priceless treasure. When producers go to harvest the olives, they merely take a piece of bread with them. They eat some of the olives that they have collected, still in their natural state without having been treated, with the bread that they have brought with them. These olives are a totally natural product which need no salt or other chemical substances to take away their bitterness. The olives lose their bitterness on the trees.

*Bread and wine. A detail from the icon "the Last Supper" by the Cretan icon painter Michael Damaskinos (16th c.)*

# CRETAN COOKING:
## The feeling of authenticity

Cretan food is different from other types of cuisine because it does not try to mix flavours, even though it uses various ingredients to make the daily food.

Each ingredient retains its own identity and taste as part of the gastronomical composition. No ingredient covers the flavour of another. All the flavours come together harmoniously in a dish and show a fine balance in taste which is characteristic of Cretan cooking.

Cretan food is a way of life; simple, basic, without over spicing and without a distortion of taste, so quite delicious! Combined in this simplicity is a creativeness of the housewife who has in her hands, centuries of experience and who never counts out or weighs ingredients. If she is asked how much flour is needed to make a certain dish, she will reply, "as much as is needed". This is an unfailing method for success even if it cannot be believed by those who prefer set amounts.

It is pure fantasy that counts most in traditional Cretan cooking. A Cretan might eat greens or pulses every day but he never eats the same food. He has found a way of enjoying new and tasty dishes. This is one of the main characteristics of Greek cuisine. Perhaps Crete merely shows a more intense style of this method due to the variety of ingredients which are used.

In areas where animals are bred, such as in the mountainous regions in the prefecture of Chania, dairy products play an important role in the cuisine. There are not only the wonderful pies filled with cheese or myzithra, but the "kreatotourta" or meat pie which

is quite impressive, along with the courgette pie and the dishes which use the tasty yoghurt of the area. But do not be fooled into believing that these dishes are served on a daily basis by the residents of the area. These particular dishes are made for feast days or special occasions. It must not also be forgotten that the housewife does not have unlimited time to spend in the kitchen.

## OLIVE OIL

More than 35.000.000 olive trees are cultivated on Crete today. Not only do they cover the needs of the inhabitants, but large quantities are exported abroad. The Cretan is well familiarized with the consumption of olive oil. Even in traditional Cretan sweets, neither butter nor refined oil nor seed oil is used, only olive oil! This oil is also used for frying. Recent studies have shown how sensible this is, as olive oil can resist heat at high temperatures much more than the other oils, it does not become oxidized and it remains healthy. It can be used 5-6 times for frying.

Cretan olive oil is made up of a high proportion of excellent quality oil. The natural juice of the olive makes up 90% of the end product, which is attained by natural or mechanical

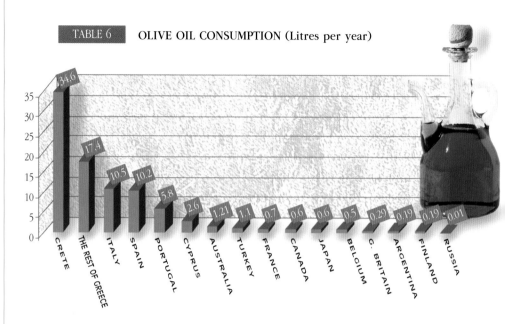

TABLE 6    OLIVE OIL CONSUMPTION (Litres per year)

CRETE 34.6 · THE REST OF GREECE 17.4 · ITALY 10.5 · SPAIN 10.2 · PORTUGAL 5.8 · CYPRUS 2.6 · AUSTRALIA 1.21 · TURKEY 1.1 · FRANCE 0.7 · CANADA 0.6 · JAPAN 0.6 · BELGIUM 0.5 · G. BRITAIN 0.29 · ARGENTINA 0.19 · FINLAND 0.19 · RUSSIA 0.01

methods, and without any chemical or other processes. Cretan olive oil does not need to be processed.

The inhabitants of the island consume the largest amounts of olive oil in the world! Statistics in studies which have been carried out in the last few years have shown this difference.

*Warning!* All the medical studies which have been conducted so far, have referred to the great consumption of olive oil, but only extra virgin olive oil. This natural juice of the olive contains not only oleic acid (the main substance of olive oil), but also a large variety of other substances which are looked upon today as vital for good health. Refined or processed olive oil is entirely another matter as it is a product of chemical procedures and so loses many of its original, valuable substances. When buying olive oil, take care to read the label. It should state that it is "extra virgin olive oil". This precious product is what has afforded the Cretans good health and long life!

Olive oil has been seen to have an effect on a large range of diseases. It helps to reduce cholesterol LDL (it only increases HDL which is known as the "good cholesterol"), it reduces the triglycerides of the blood and protects against cardiovascular diseases. It aids the lowering of blood pressure, both diastolic and systolic, so reducing the chances of strokes. Moreover, it has anti-oxidative agents which help to protect against cancer. It helps in the functioning of the liver, and combined with the consumption of vegetables, can be seen to protect against cancer of the gastrointestinal tract. It should also be mentioned that olive oil is perfect in the diet of someone who suffers from diabetes. All in all, studies are frequently published which prove the undoubtable value of olive oil and furthermore, advise the use of this oil in maintaining good health.

# MORE INFORMATION:
# A BOOK ABOUT
# OLIVE OIL

In one of our handy books (published by KARMANOR), entitled, "Olive Oil, the secret of good health", you can find a complete study of this wonderful product. The book contains information about its history, its biological value, advice on its correct use, facts about edible olives, as well as 150 recipes for main courses, starters and sweets which use olive oil as a basic ingredient.

# OLIVE OIL
# AT BREAKFAST!

Try replacing the butter which you usually use at breakfast. You can use a recipe which was enjoyed by the Cretans in the old days: pour a little olive oil on a slice of wholemeal bread.

You might even want to choose a flavoured oil which has been scented naturally with herbs or aromatic greens.

You can flavour your own oil by leaving a sprig of a herb in the bottle with the olive oil for two weeks.

In the old days on Crete, pure olive oil was drizzled on the bread and then oregano and salt were sprinkled on top. It is a wonderful breakfast which is full of good health!

The traditional Cretan breakfast might also have included a herbal tea, such as Dittany of Crete, which was frequently praised by doctors in ancient times, fresh fruit, olives and on some occasions the Cretans were known to dunk a dry rusk in some red wine.

The bread was always black, wholemeal and usually made from barley flour.

# DIFFERENCES BETWEEN THE CRETAN AND THE MEDITERRANEAN DIET

There may be very similar conditions in almost all the areas of the Mediterranean but it is Crete that stands out amongst them. This has been proved by the medical studies (see Tables 1, 2 and 3) which clearly show that the Cretans have the best level of health (in stark contrast to the other areas studied) in comparison to the inhabitants of the other Mediterranean areas studied.

This Cretan dietary model includes the exclusive use of olive oil, along with a large consumption of fruit and vegetables but little meat. The differences in the amounts are shown in Table 5 where the variations in the amounts of different foods consumed by the Cretans and those inhabitants of the other areas in the Mediterranean that were studied are quite obvious.

*Saint Euphrosynos, a Cretan saint! A contemporary icon from the convent of Chrysopighi in Chania.*

# CRETAN COOKING
## (Introductory note)

The development of Cretan cooking right up to the middle of the 20th century is typical of a way of cooking which relies basically on its own produce. The products of agriculture, livestock and fishing, were, until the last few decades, the basic source of nourishment in Cretan households and in local cooking.

Cretan cooking has its roots way back in ancient times. Although there aren't enough sources to give us a complete picture of the eating habits of the Cretans, we do know today that basically, Cretan cooking hasn't changed since Minoan times: indeed there have been very few additions to the products which were familiar to the prehistoric inhabitants of the island.

We know for a fact that Minoans used olive oil just as Cretans do today, that they stored their cereals and that they enriched their meals with the pure wine from the extensive Cretan vineyards and with the fish caught in

*Cleaning wild greens in Vorizia, a village on the slopes of Psiloreitis.*

the boundless seas that surround the island. We also know that many of the local products brought the Minoans, who were remarkable merchants, riches and power, enabling them to control business and navigation in all the Mediterranean and perhaps even beyond, along other sea routes, if we are to believe more daring scholars. It seems that most of the products for export were agricultural, though herbs were also very much in demand.

In classical times, Cretan cooking doesn't seem to have differed much from cooking in the other regions of Greece. Our sources for this period are mainly Athenian, including however, some scanty information about Crete. Apparently, cooking at that time had a general character all over Greece, though of course with some important local differences. Sweet and sour sauces, later on thought to be of French inspiration, have their origin in Greek antiquity, as is the case with many specific tastes predominant nowadays in European cooking. A more profound study of eating habits in ancient Greece would be of great interest as it would show the innovative contribution classical Greece has made to the craft of cooking.

In the following years, Cretan cooking was enriched through contacts with other civilisations and the successive conquests of the island brought about exchange and interchange in eating habits. It is a well-known fact today that the Roman ruling class appreciated Cretan culinary products, especially the wine (the Lyktios wine and the wine from Sitia were much sought after even at the palace court).

Important innovations took place during the long period when Crete was part of the Byzantine Empire. It was the time when the famous Byzantine cooking was developing and Crete contributed greatly with its own cultural experience in the field. It is not accidental that most Byzantine dishes we find in literary texts are still to be found nowadays on Crete with the same names. As a Byzantine province, Crete was outstanding in its contribution to this civilisation. And later on, after the breakup of the Byzantine Empire and its conquest by the Ottomans (1453), Crete became the cultural capital of the orthodox world.

Many Byzantine scholars came to live in Chandax (known today as Heraklion) after 1453, bringing, together with all their belongings, the eating habits of Constantinople. During this period, the island belonged to the Venetian Republic and the Venetian dignitaries, who settled in the cities and in luxurious villas in the villages and brought their own eating habits to their new country. Different civilisations met and Crete became the melting pot or crossroads for their different styles of cooking, which once assimilated and incorporated, became part of the traditional Cretan cuisine. It is important to remember that traditional Cretan cooking formed the basis of all the developments that followed.

The list of the products which were exported from Crete during the Venetian period are of particular interest. Among them we find the wonderful Cretan wine (famous throughout the whole civilised world of the time), honey, olive oil, cheese and other products.

The Turkish occupation of the island (1669) had no influence whatsoever on traditional Cretan cooking. The only "influence" which can be traced is the Turkish names given to several dishes which, of course, existed long before the Ottomans. We must not be fooled by these names.

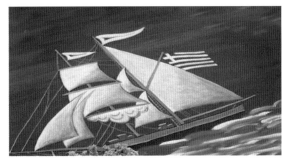

Cretan cooking is the direct and natural result of a civilisation which was developed by those people living permanently on Cretan land, tilling the soil and having at their disposal all the required supplies to shape their eating habits.

The Turkish domination of the island suspended all cultural activity and reduced the economy to its primitive form of subsistence farming. In the first years of the Turkish occupation, Crete lost its ascendancy in commerce and trade. All this had an immediate effect on the development of cooking. Poverty and indigence forced the inhabitants of the island to look for easier and more accessible solutions to the problem of food. But even then the basis of Cretan cooking remained unchanged as is shown in the sophisticated dishes cooked for feasts and in the baking of a great variety of sacred breads, which are difficult to prepare, requiring both knowledge and experience. When the Turkish domination ended in 1898, new eating habits were developed and one can observe reciprocal influences in the ways of cooking of different peoples. The Cretan cooking in towns was, at that time, very much under the influence of the customs in Asia Minor, due to the close contact that existed at that time between

*Representation of a supper in Cretan Rennaissance icon painting. Detail from the icon "the last Supper" by the Cretan icon painter Michael Damaskinos (16th c.)*

the inhabitants of the island and those of Asia Minor. On the other hand, cooking in the villages retained its ancient properties, even after the Union of Crete with the rest of Greece (1913).

In the next few decades Cretan households continued to get their supplies from local produce with the result that Cretan cookery became exclusively seasonal. Some products were prepared in the spring time, others during the summer and others in winter and all these products retained their full flavour, bringing the fragrance of each season.

Close contact with Egypt, areas of Asia Minor and the Middle East enabled the Cretans to get large supplies of spices which they widely used in their cooking. It is, however, important to remember, that capers, oregano and other such local products were never replaced but continue to be widely used, just as were native herbs for the preparation of wonderful tisanes. The creative abilities of the local population are inseparably linked to the basic virtues still present in Cretan cooking. There are indeed very few plants and parts of the plant that are not used in cooking.

The marrow plant not only gives us delicious courgettes, which can be served in a salad (boiled) or can be cooked in many different ways, either stuffed, fried or in omelets, but at the same time the Cretan cook also uses the flowers of the plant (which are indeed very much prized on the island) or the tender shoots which are also cooked.

In the same manner, the leaves of the vine are eaten stuffed, while the tender shoots give an excellent, rather sour, taste; grape juice is an admirable natural sweetener, and of course raisins are used either for sweets or in ordinary food (Cretan "omathies" and "tzoulamas" are famous dishes with raisins).

And then, there is also the olive tree, enhancing the beauty of extensive areas of the island while offering priceless olive oil and olives which can be eaten both raw and cooked. The oil always was, and continues to be, the basis of Cretan cooking. This outstanding product has been praised by scientists for its excellent effects on one's health and general physical well-being and is always present in Cretan cooking, whether raw or cooked, with a variety of foods.

Animal fats were never widely used on the island, except at Christmas time when every household had a pig slaughtered and its meat was used in the preparation of various dishes. But this was during a very short period and had no serious effect on the general diet.

Abundant greens, pulses, cereals and meat, both from local livestock and game, are to be found among other select products used in Cretan cooking. Cheese was also profusely used in stock-raising regions. In many of these, dairy products enrich cooking, giving the food a special taste. Assorted meatpies -meat pastries in Chania- provide an excellent example of cheese-made products.

Largely, the same kind of cooking is to be found all over the island, though of course there are important variations which set off the specific ways of life and household managing of each place.

The "kallitsounia" and the "myzithropites", for example, are to be found everywhere on the island, yet the ones from Sitia, called "anevata", differ from the "agnopites" of Heraklion, from the "sarikopites" of Anoyia and from the "sfakianopites" in Sfakia. The use of the same (or very similar) ingredients result in different tastes...

These changes are always due to the nature of each place and its people. The inhabitants of Sfakia did not prepare sauces because the food had to be taken to the mountains where the stock-farmers lived and the conveyance of liquid food was difficult, whereas meatpies and other typical dishes from the mountain regions were easier to carry.

In this book, local specialities are set off against the more general background of Cretan cooking. In many cases, several different ways of preparing the same dishes are mentioned, after long and careful research of all the regions on the island...

At the beginning of each chapter, an introductory note gives the historical and folkloric background and individual notes are given when a specific dish has historical or folkloric value.

*A young Cretan boy selling bread rings (the tasty small bread rings with sesame seeds which accompany Greek breakfast). A postcard from the early 20th c.*

# MEAT
## Historical review

A brilliant civilization developed on Crete 4,000 years ago which left a great number of significant monuments on the island. It is known as the Minoan civilization, named after Minos, the legendary king of Crete. Important information has been saved about nutrition during those times. It has been proved that they used olive oil in cooking, while meat traces have been detected in clay pots by chemical and other analyses.

However, meat was not consumed every day; it was usually connected with the rituals. This continued long later, until after 1450 B. C. The following text belongs to the French professor Paul Faure:

*"The peasants and the people working in the palaces had frugal, vegetarian meals. They consumed and were paid in grains, -wheat or barley-, dried figs and olives in brine. A little goat, beef or pork meat was consumed only on feast days"*

*(Paul Faure, "La vie quotidienne au temps de Minos")*

In ancient Greece, it was more of a dish for the well-off, especially the landowners who bred oxen, pigs, goats and sheep on their estates; though the poor also had meat, but not very often.

These habits affected the diet of the Cretans later on.

Demands of the church regarding fasting which were known in the ancient religion of the Greeks, brought about a dietary prototype whereby the diet relied heavily on the consumption of naturally produced products. The orthodox church banned the eating of meat and in general, any food which came from animals for long periods of time (40 days before Christmas, seven weeks before Easter, 15 days before the celebration of the Assumption on 15th August, every Wednesday and Friday during the year and there were still some other short periods of fasting). In all, certain foods were forbidden for one third of the year! Until the beginning of the 20th century, Cretans ate meat only a few times every

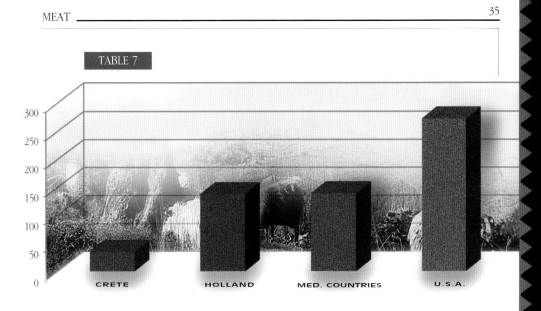

**MEAT CONSUMPTION - STUDY OF THE SEVEN COUNTRIES (grams per day)**

year and then, only on feast days; Christmas, Easter and 15th August as well as on social occasions such as weddings and baptisms. The meat was the official dish, a dish of prestige.

Medical studies which emphasise the value of the Cretan diet as a precious ally in the attainment and maintenance of good health, show that these islanders consume less meat in comparison to the other groups that were studied. In particular, on average, during the 1960s, each Cretan consumed only 25% of the meat which was eaten by the populations in the other Mediterranean areas and 12.8% less meat than those people studied in USA.

# How the Cretans cook meat

E ven today, Cretans eat meat which mainly comes from small animals. Traditionally, the Cretans rarely ate meat from bulls or cows, and pork was only slightly more popular. Still today, mutton is the Cretans' favourite meat. The sheep are bred on the island and roam freely. This meat is nearly always cooked with greens, vegetables or pulses. These form impressive combinations with fantastic tastes so that each product retains its own characteristic flavour.

*WARNING: The Cretan diet is not only vegetarian. It is merely based on a large consumption of greens, vegetables, pulses and on the whole, products with natural origins, but it does not exclude certain foods which come from animals. It is just that the animal based products are eaten less frequently and in smaller amounts.*
*Thus, the human body is not denied anything.*

# TRADITIONAL MEAT DISHES

On Crete, pork is traditionally eaten at Christmas and lamb at Easter. During the rest of the year, meat from small animals is consumed, such as goat, sheep, rabbit and poultry. All these animals are to be found ranging freely on the island.

# CHRISTMAS PORK

The slaughter of pigs is a national Greek custom with Roman origins: pigs were offered to placate the gods Chronus and Demeter and invoke their help for good crops. The custom survived into the Christian era and is still to be found in most Cretan villages. Rural families slaughter their pig on Christmas Eve, which ends a period of long fasting: from the 15th of November to the 25th of December. During all this time, the Cretan of old ate greens, which were abundant after the first rains, pulses, cereals and sometimes fish. In a way, it was a period for a natural wholesome diet, such as is recommended nowadays by dieticians. Christmas pork gave everyone the chance to eat lots of meat, after having refrained from eating any for so many days.

# Brawn "Tsiladia"

*"Tsiladia" or brawn, was prepared using the head and the feet of the pig on the day after Christmas. Left to set in an earthenware pot (the cold weather of the season helped), it was served on New Year's Day. It was an indispensable addition to the New Year's feast.*
*Today, this delicacy is prepared all the year round.*

*Tsilathia (Brawn)*

pig's head
or 2 kilos of pork meat (boneless)
pig's trotters
the peel of an orange
1 cup orange
or bitter orange juice
1 cup lemon juice
1/2 cup vinegar
salt, cumin, pepper
a little nutmeg

After cleaning the head and the trotters thoroughly, boil them in salted water until properly cooked, at least two hours and a half. Remove the pot from the heat and when the meat is cold enough, remove the bones. (The ears remain as such; they are one of the best parts of the "tsiladia").

Strain the broth and add some water to have about 7 cups of liquid in all. Add the boneless meat chopped up and the juices (orange or bitter orange and lemon), the vinegar, the orange peel and the spices. Bring the mixture to the boil, remove from the fire and let it cool.

Divide the brawn into several earthen-ware bowls (according to the quantity prepared), taking care that the liquid covers all the pieces.

Put the brawn in the refrigerator to set and keep it there. With a spoon, remove the fat from the surface, before serving.

## "Apaki" Smoked meat

"Apaki" is a smoked meat, known since Byzantine times and very common on Crete. It was made with the tender meat around the kidneys. A delicacy in Venetian times, it was to be found in most Cretan households.

The meat used for "apaki" is cut in strips and left in a bowl with vinegar for 3-4 days. Then it is salted, peppered and hung over the fire-place. Several, freshly gathered Cretan aromatic herbs (oregano, sage, bay leaves and others) are then burnt and the fire is covered with the ashes so as to make it smoke profusely. The meat is cooked in this fashion with the smoke and can be kept for many weeks.

## EASTER LAMB

After a long period of fasting which has lasted seven weeks before the celebration of Easter, the Cretans, like the rest of the Greeks, enjoy a rich meal with lamb.

In many areas in Greece, lamb is roasted on the spit as a whole and is an extremely tasty Easter dish which is enjoyed by families and friends as they come together to have fun on this special celebration.

On Easter Sunday on Crete, the traditional dish is not lamb on the spit but lamb cooked with vegetables.

The first meal after the forty days of Lent is a delicious and yet light meat soup which is made from liver, intestines and aromatic local greens. It is known all over Greece as "magiritsa". This soup is usually eaten at night on Easter Saturday, after having returned from church where the ceremony of the resurrection of Christ was observed.

## LAMB ON THE SPIT: AN ANCIENT CUSTOM

Shepherds on the mountains of Madara and Psiloritis love this dish. They cook it when they shear their sheep (in May) or when they have guests up in the mountains.

The way they do it is not only interesting but almost ritual. The youngest shepherd clears an appropriate place, discarding stones and bushes. He then digs a small hole in the ground in which he lights a fire, placing stones all around the hole to keep the spit in place.

This is reminiscent of ancient Greece, as in those days they dug exactly the same holes, which they called "vothroi". There, they made their offerings to the gods of the Underworld!

So it is, that ever since, or perhaps even earlier, lamb on the spit or "ofto" has been the Greeks' favourite meal. The shepherds up on Psiloritis don't wait till the coals are red, as they do in the rest of Greece, to cook their lamb. They skewer big chunks on the spit which has been prepared right there and allow it to cook at the temperature given off by the burning wood. They are, it must be said, very impatient.

There's an explanation for this impatience: it goes back to the time of bondage.

Meat on the spit requires fire and therefore smoke, which betrays the spot where the fire has been lit. The old time rebels, called "chainis", were always in a hurry, always on the run...

And what about the spit? It too has its origins in ancient Greece. It looks like one of the spears the warriors of ancient Greece used, not only in fighting, but to cook their own meat...

# Lamb on the spit «ofto»

An Easter meal, well established all over Greece.

Some regions of the country, like Roumeli, claim the origin of this custom. In Crete, it varies slightly from region to region. In most cases, the lamb is not cooked in one piece, but in chunks and over coals in a shallow hole in the ground.

In those regions where the lamb is cooked in one piece, it is cleaned and basted in lemon juice and oregano. Sometimes the "knisari" is twisted around it, and the greasy membrane melts into the meat as it cooks, giving it a more savoury taste.

A long time ago, the spit was a long, thin piece of wood about 2 meters long.

Today there are special metal ones, some are even electric and turn automatically.

Put the lamb on the spit and tie it firmly; then turn the spit constantly, ensuring there is no flame, until the lamb is cooked. While cooking, baste it with olive oil. When chunks of meat come off the bone, the meat is ready.

The whole preparation of the Easter lamb is like a liturgy, a real feast with music from lyres (Cretan traditional instrument), songs, dances, red dyed eggs, special Easter cheese pies and a general feeling of happiness.

# «Tzoulamas» Rice-filled pie

*This is an essentially carnival dish, traditionally served as a dessert. It is cooked in different ways in central Crete.*

*The following recipe is prepared in the area of Messara.*

### The dough:
*(You can also use commercial "filo", a paper-thin pastry)*

half a kilo of flour
3 tbsps olive oil
1 teasp. salt
1 cup water

### The **stuffing**:
300 grams liver
2 cups rice
1 cup raisins (sultanas)

1 cup pistachios or almonds
(in some regions chestnuts
or walnuts are used)
1/2 cup olive oil
salt
pepper
cinnamon
1 cup sugar
1 cup chicken broth or milk

Chop the liver, add salt and pepper and brown it in 3 tbsps olive oil.

Add 5 cups water and boil the rice for 10 minutes.
A little before removing the pan from the fire, add the nuts, the raisins and 1/2 cup sugar. Stir.
Prepare the dough and divide into three three parts.

Oil a baking pan, open one sheet of pastry, place it on the borrom of the baking pan and sprinkle with sugar and cinnamon. Spread half the stuffing.

In the same manner put on a second sheet of pastry and spread the second half of the stuffing, covering it with the last sheet of pastry.
Pour the remaining oil and the chicken broth or the milk over the whole dish, sprinkling it once again with sugar and cinnamon.
Bake in a medium oven until the pastry turns golden, about one hour.

# Poached goat - Wedding spaghetti

1 kilo goat or sheep
1/2 kilo spaghetti No 6
salt
1 cup grated "anthotyros"
(see chapter on "Cheeses")

Cook and strain the meat as in the following recipe. Add more water to the pot to have 6 cups in all and a little salt. Bring to the boil and cook the spaghetti on high temperature for about 10 minutes.
Serve after 5 minutes, sprinkled with grated "anthotyros" or another cheese.

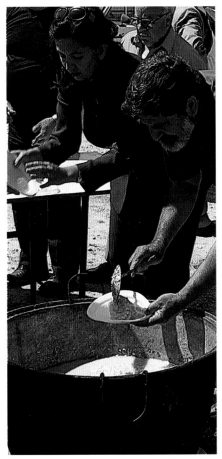

*Handing out rice pilaff at a feast in Sfakia*

rature at the beginning and skim off the scum from the surface. Increase the temperature to medium, cook the meat and strain.

Measure out the stock and get it to the boil. Measure the rice and cook it in the stock (1 cup of rice for 3 of stock). When the rice is cooked, add salt and the lemon juice and take the pot off the heat. Melt the butter and pour it over the rice.

# Meat with honey

People in western and central Crete used to and still do to this day, serve meat with honey!

They do it with poached or grilled meat, usually lamb or kid, which, once cooked, they baste with honey. One or two tablespoons of honey are enough for each portion.

If you like peculiar tastes and the combination of something sweet with salty foods, then you should try this dish. You will find it interesting, especially if you use the herbal Cretan honey, which smells of sage or other herbs.

# Pilaff from the region of Sfakia

1 kilo of a 2-year old lamb and
a chicken
1 kilo of rice
2 tbsps «staka»
(fresh goat's butter)
or any butter
5 tbsps lemon juice
salt

Wash and cut the meat into portions, put it in a pot and cover with water and a little salt. Boil on low tempe-

*Meatpie*

# Meat-and-vegetable pie

The **dough**:
1/2 kg flour
1/2 cup olive oil
1/2 cup water
1 teasp. salt
The **filling**:
1 kg pork meat
1 kg greens
(spinach, fennel, parsley, mint, spring onion, leeks etc.)
1/2 cup olive oil
salt, pepper

Wash the greens, chop them roughly, add salt and brown them in half the oil for 15 minutes.
Wash and chop the meat, add salt and pepper and brown it, too, in the rest of the olive oil for half an hour.
Prepare the dough with the above ingredients and roll out two sheets. Spread one sheet of pastry on an oiled baking pan; on this spread half the amount of greens, continue with the meat and on top, spread the rest of the greens. Cover with the second sheet, dab with olive oil and bake in a moderate heat for about one hour.

# Meatpie

*It is one of the favourite Easter dishes in western Crete, although it can be prepared on other occassions as well. It is a dish of the mountainous regions and has a special, wonderful taste.*

The **dough**:
1/2 kilo of flour
1/2 cup milk or yoghurt
1/2 cup olive oil
1/2 teasp. salt

**Stuffing:**
1 kilo of lean meat
(lamb, goat or calf)
1 kilo of cheese
(50% soft anthotyros
and 50% sour myzithra,
see the chapter on cheeses)
3 tbsps of "staka"
(fresh goat's butter) or olive oil
salt, pepper, cinnamon powder
1 tbsp finely chopped mint

*Meat with green beans*

Cut the meat into serving portions, wash it and boil it in water for 1 hour. Take it out of the pot, let it cool and chop into very small cubes. Add salt, pepper and cinnamon.

Prepare the dough with the above ingredients and divide it in two.

Roll out one half and spread the sheet on an oiled baking pan. Put half the "myzithra", keeping it 2 cm from the edge of the pastry. Sprinkle with mint. On top, put the meat and then the rest of the cheese. Finally, spread the "staka" or a little olive oil and cover with the other sheet of pastry. Join the edges of the bottom and top layers together pressing them tightly with your fingers.. Dab with egg, sprinkle with

sesame seeds and bake the meatpie in a medium oven for about one hour.

# Meat with fresh green beans

> 1/2 cup olive oil
> 1 onion or 1-2 leeks, chopped
> 1 kilo of meat
> (either lamb, beef or pork)
> 1 kilo of green beans
> 1/2 kilo of ripe tomatoes,
> finely chopped
> salt and pepper

Wash and clean the beans: cut off the tips and remove the fibres from both sides.

Brown the onion or the leeks in the oil and then add the meat cut into cubes. Brown the meat for 10-15 minutes, add half the tomatoes, 1 cup water and simmer for 30 minutes. Add the beans, the rest of the tomatoes, salt, pepper and some water. Simmer till cooked, about an hour.

# Meat and aubergine stew

1 kilo meat
(preferably pork or veal)
1/2 cup olive oil
1 onion, finely chopped
1 kilo long aubergines
100 ml white wine
1/2 kilo finely chopped
tomatoes
2-3 cloves garlic,
finely chopped
salt, pepper, 1 cinnamon stick

Cut the meat into cubes, wash and brown in a pot with the olive oil and the onion. Add the wine and after 5 minutes, the tomatoes, the garlic and 2 cups water. Let it simmer until cooked, about an hour and a half.

In the meantime, cut the aubergines into medium pieces, add salt and let them lose their bitterness. Rinse and drain them and fry them slightly. Add them to the pot and simmer for a further 10 minutes.

# Meat and cauliflower

1 kilo meat (pork or veal)
1/2 cup olive oil
2 medium onions, finely chopped
1 medium cauliflower
100 ml wine (optional)
1/2 kilo pulped tomatoes
salt, pepper

Wash meat and cut into cubes.
Heat the olive oil in a pot and brown the onion and the meat turning frequently on all sides. Stir in wine, tomato and 2 cups water. Simmer for about an hour and a half, until meat is almost tender and add cauliflower cut into florets, salt and pepper.
Simmer for 20 more minutes without stirring the cauliflower, only shaking it back and forth.

# Meat with chickpeas

*This is a wedding dish in many parts of Crete. In the villages of Messara it is cooked the day before the wedding and, with large quantities of red wine, is served to the guests. In the village of Anoyia, when weddings were on Sundays, this dish was prepared on the Thursday before, which was when the bridegroom's gifts ("kaniskia") were taken to the bride's house. On this occasion the bride's family served this meal, with lots of red wine.*

**Ingredients:**
1 kilo of meat
(preferably pork or veal)
1/2 kilo of chickpeas
1/2 cup of olive oil
2 onions, finely chopped
1/2 kilo of finely chopped
tomatoes
salt, pepper

Cut the meat into cubes and brown it with the onion in a pot. Add the tomato and let it simmer for a while. Strain the chickpeas (which have been soaking in water since the evening before) and put them in the pot. Cover with water, add salt and pepper and simmer until cooked.

*Right:*
*Dried beans and meat*

*Youvetsi, meat with very small pasta*

## Dried beans and meat

To be cooked like chickpeas and meat with the addition of two tbsps of chopped parsley and a hot pepper is optional.

## Meat with very small pasta "Youvetsi"

*This dish was not common in the old days among the rural population of the island. What is more, in most villages, it was almost unknown until the last few decades. However, it is a very popular dish through-out the rest of Greece.*

*Shortly before World War I, it figures in handwritten recipe notebooks of the urban population of Crete. It soon became very popular and during the 60's and 70's, when each family took their Sunday food to the* bakery of the neighbourhood to be cooked, youvetsi was the commonest dish.

**Ingredients:**
1 kilo of meat
(veal, lamb or chicken)
1/2 cup olive oil
4 or 5 ripe tomatoes
1/2 kilo of very small pasta
(like grains of rice)
salt and pepper
1 cup of grated cheese

Cut the meat into small portions, wash and put in a tin or earthenware casserole (you can also divide it into several small earthenware dishes). Pour the pulped tomatoes over the meat, add salt and pepper. Then add the oil and a cup of water and bake the meat in a moderate oven. About half an hour before it is cooked, add the pasta with 5 cups of hot water, mixing it well with the tomato and adding some salt. Serve sprinkled with grated cheese.

# Meat soup yalitiki

*This dish has its origins in Venetian times. It was a soup cooked in the coastal areas of Crete.*

1 kilo veal
1/2 kilo finely chopped onions
4 tbsps olive oil
salt

Cut meat into stewing pieces, wash it, put it in a large pot and cover with water. Add salt and simmer, skimming off the scum from the surface.
When the meat is nearly tender, in about one and a half hours, stir in the onion which you have browned in the olive oil. Boil for another 20 minutes.

# Traditional veal stew

1 kilo of veal
1/2 cup of oil
1 kilo of onions, roughly chopped
2 cloves of garlic
2-3 bay leaves
1 cup of red wine
2 tbsps of vinegar
3 tomatoes, finely chopped
salt, pepper, cumin
1 cinnamon stick

Wash meat and cut into stewing pieces. Heat the oil in a pot and sauté the meat

for a few minutes, turning frequently on all sides. Add the onions, the lbay leaves and the garlic and sauté for a few more minutes. Pour in the wine to cover the meat. Add the tomato, salt, pepper, cumin and the cinnamon stick and let it cook very slowly until most liquid has evaporated and the meat is tender.

# Veal in lemon juice

1 kilo of veal
1/2 cup olive oil
1 onion finely chopped
100 ml white wine
salt, pepper
2 tbsps of flour
70 ml lemon juice

Wash meat and cut into cubes.
Heat oil in a skillet and brown the meat on all sides. Add the onion, brown it and then pour in the wine. Add salt, pepper and 2 cups water and simmer until most of the liquid has been absorbed.
Dissolve the flour in the lemon juice and add to the pot. Simmer for another 10 minutes and then turn off the heat.

# Beef stew with potatoes

1 kilo beef
1,5 kilos potatoes
1 finely chopped onion
1/2 cup of olive oil
1/2 kilo grated tomatoes
1 spoonful of flour
salt, pepper

Wash meat, cut into cubes and brown in the olive oil with the onion and the flour. Stir in the chopped tomatoes, salt, pepper and cover with water. Cook for about an hour and then add the potatoes, cut into slices. Boil for another half hour adding a little more salt and water, if needed.

# Baked meat balls with potatoes

750 grams minced meat
250 grams stale bread, soaked in water and slightly squeezed
1 egg slightly beaten
1 medium onion, grated
1/2 cup finely chopped onion
salt, pepper
3-4 medium potatoes
For the **sauce**: 5 tbsps olive oil
1 finely chopped onion
1/2 kilo finely chopped tomatoes
1 teasp. thyme or oregano
salt, pepper

In a large bowl, combine meat with bread, egg, onion, parsley, salt and pepper.
Prepare the sauce; heat the oil in a pan and sauté the onion until translucent. Stir in tomatoes, salt, pepper, thyme or oregano and 1 cup water and simmer for 10 minutes.
Peel the potatoes, cut into slices, sprinkle with salt and place on the bottom of an oiled baking tin in one layer. Shape quite large meat balls and place on top of the potatoes. Pour the sauce over the meat balls and bake in preheated oven for about an hour.

# Meat balls (keftethes) in egg-lemon sauce

1 kilo of minced meat
1 cup bread crumbs
1 grated onion
1/2 cup finely chopped parsley
1/2 cup grated cheese
2 egg whites
salt, pepper
oil and flour for the frying
The **sauce**:
2 or 3 onions
3 tbsps vinegar
100 ml milk
2 yokes
2 tbsps olive oil
2 tbsps flour

Prepare the mixture by combining all the ingredients together.
Shape the meat balls, roll in flour and fry lightly. (Alternatively, they can be baked in the oven).
Prepare the **sauce:** chop the onions and put them in a saucepan with 1/2 cup water. As soon as they have absorbed the water, add the olive oil and brown them, then pour in the vinegar. Add 2 more cups water, bring to the boil and put in the meat balls. Let them simmer for 15 minutes.
Beat the yokes, add the milk, a little salt, 1 tbsp. of flour and a few tbsps of the stock. Add to the meat, stir and turn off the heat.

# "Moussakas"

*Nobody knows exactly when this savoury and tasty dish became common on Crete, though there are recipes for Moussakas from the end of the 19th century. It was a common dish among the town dwellers of Heraklion and Chania, and by the beginning of the*

*20th century it was also popular in larger villages close to the big towns. But for the families living in the country, it proved a difficult dish to prepare, because it requires a lot of time and a great many cooking utensils.*

*It's said that moussakas is the link between popular and sophisticated cooking. Although there aren't any sources to establish the date when this dish first appeared, moussakas figures in the oldest recipe notebooks of Crete: therefore it may be assumed that it has been made on the island since, at least, the last quarter of the 19th century.*

### Ingredients:

courgettes, aubergines, potatoes
(1 kilo of each kind)
1 kilo of minced meat
4 tbsps olive oil
2 finely chopped onions
100 ml wine
4-5 pulped tomatoes
3 eggs
1 cup grated cheese
salt, pepper

1 cup bread crumbs
For the **sauce**:
8 tbsps flour
4 tbsps butter or olive oil
2 litres milk, 2 eggs
salt, pepper, nutmeg

Brown the meat and onions in oil, pour in the wine, add the tomatoes, salt and pepper and cook for about half an hour. Then, stir in the beaten eggs, the cheese and the bread crumbs.

Slightly fry the courgettes, the aubergines, the potatoes, all cut in large slices. (These can also be baked with a little oil in the oven, to make a lighter moussakas; one can also use only aubergines or only courgettes).

Butter a baking pan, sprinkle it with bread crumbs and alternate a layer of potatoes with a layer of minced meat, a layer of aubergines and then a layer of meat, a layer of courgettes and again meat.

Prepare the **sauce:** melt the butter or the olive oil; when very hot add the flour and stir till it gains a little colour. Add the milk and stir till it thickens. Finally, add the beaten eggs, the salt, the pepper and the nutmeg.

Pour the white sauce on the dish, sprinkle with cheese and cook the moussakas in the oven until it turns golden brown.

# Small meat pasties (kimathopitakia)

**The dough:** 1 cup olive oil
2 eggs
1 cup milk
1 teasp. salt
1 teasp. baking powder
flour (about 1 kilo)
**The stuffing:** 1 kilo minced meat
1 onion
4 tbsps olive oil
salt, pepper and cinnamon

Prepare the dough with the above ingredients.

Brown the meat in the oil with the chopped onion, salt, pepper and cinnamon.

Roll out the dough and cut out 10 cm circles. Put 1 tbsp meat on each piece, and shape semi-circular pasties.

You can also make "sarikopites" by cutting the dough in long strips and rolling up the minced meat in them like a turban ("sariki", a turban, was also the local name given to the head-dress Cretan men used to wear -and some still do). Fry them in very hot oil. Serve while still hot.

# Meat balls filled with potato purée

*This dish was commonly cooked in the village of Aghos Myronas, and maybe in other villages of the province of Malevizi as well.*

**Ingredients:**
half a kilo of minced meat

1 kilo of potatoes
6 tbsps olive oil
1 finely chopped onion
1-2 eggs
1/2 cup grated cheese
1/2 cup flour or rusk crumbs
salt, pepper

Sauté the minced meat with the onion in the olive oil. Add salt and pepper.

Boil the potatoes, make a potato mash, add salt, a little pepper, the cheese, the eggs and the rusk crumbs or flour. Shape this mixture into small balls and dig a hole in the middle of each: insert 1 teasp. of the cooked meat, close the hole carefully with the potato mash and roll the "keftethes" in flour before deep-frying them in very hot oil.

Instead of using flour, the meat-cum-potato balls can be dipped in egg and in bread crumbs (or rusk).

# Aubergine rolls with minced meat

1 kilo aubergines
1/2 kilo minced meat
1 finely chopped onion
3 tbsps olive oil
salt, pepper
2 eggs
1 cup bread crumbs

Cut the aubergines in long slices and fry them. Put on kitchen roll to drain.

Sauté the minced meat with the olive oil, the onion, salt and pepper. Spread 1 tbsp meat on the aubergine slices and roll them up. Dip the rolls in beaten egg and in bread crumbs. Deep-fry.

(Instead of frying them, you can prepare a tomato sauce. Pour it over the rolls and bake in the oven).

*Lamb with okra*

# Lamb (or goat) with okra

1 kg meat cut into serving pieces
1 kilo okra
1/2 kilo chopped tomatoes
1/2 cup olive oil
1 chopped onion
4 tbsps vinegar
salt and pepper

Wash the okra, cut off the stems, douse with vinegar and let them stand in the sun for a couple of hours.

Brown the meat in the pot with the oil and the onion.

Add the tomatoes and 1-2 cups water and simmer till the meat is almost tender.

Then add the okra, salt, pepper, a little water if needed, and simmer for another 30-40 minutes.

# Lamb (or goat) with fennel leaves

1 kg meat cut into serving pieces
1 finely chopped onion
1 kilo fennel leaves
2 lemons
1/2 cup olive oil
salt
pepper

Brown the meat in the oil, turning it on all sides and add the chopped fennel leaves and the onion.

Pour in 2 cups water and cook for about an hour and a half.

Finally add the lemon juice, salt and pepper.

Bring back to the boil: the dish is ready.

## Lamb (or goat) in egg-lemon sauce

1 kg meat cut into serving pieces
2 or 3 spring onions
1 cup finely chopped dill
1/2 cup olive oil
1 egg, 2 lemons
salt
pepper

Brown the meat in the olive oil and add the chopped onion and dill, the salt and pepper, and 2 cups water. Simmer.

Once the meat has been cooked, prepare the egg and lemon sauce: beat the lemon juice with the eggs and add a few spoonfuls of the stock.

Remove the pot from the fire to keep the sauce from curdling, pour the mixture over the meat and stir.

## Lamb (or kid) with artichokes

Cook the meat as above, but half way through, put in the hearts of 1 kilo of artichokes (cut cross-wise, but leaving them whole). Let the food cook and at the end, pour in the egg and lemon sauce.

## Lamb (or kid) with lettuce

The same as above but replace the artichokes with 2 or 3 heads of coarsely chopped lettuce.

## Lamb (or kid) with chicories or spinach

Follow the same instructions as above with the only difference that you should boil them for 10 minutes and drain them before adding them to the meat.

*Right: Lamb with artichokes in egg-lemon sauce*

*Baked lamb with yoghurt*

# Lamb (or goat) in wine

> 1,5 kg meat cut
> in serving portions
> 5-6 tbsps olive oil
> the juice of 1 lemon
> 1-2 cups white wine
> salt, pepper

Wash meat, remove as many bones as you can, baste with lemon juice, salt and pepper and brown it in the olive oil turning it on all sides. Simmer, adding the wine, a little at a time, until it is cooked.

# Baked lamb (or goat) with yoghurt

> 1 kilo meat
> 750 grams strained yoghurt
> 4 tbsps olive oil
> 2 eggs
> 1 grated nutmeg
> juice of 1 lemon
> salt

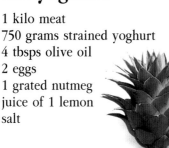

Wash the meat, cut into serving portions, baste with lemon juice, salt and 2 tbsps olive oil and place in a baking tin. Bake in the oven for about an hour and a half, take out of the oven and sprinkle with the nutmeg.

Beat the eggs with the rest of the olive oil and the yoghurt, pour the mixture over the meat and bake in the oven for another 15 minutes until it sets.

# Baked lamb (or goat) with artichockes and yoghurt

Prepare the artichokes: remove the outer leaves, trim the ends and rub with lemon juice.

Boil them in salty water for 5 minutes and, half way through, add them to the meat in the baking tin.

When both meat and artichockes are tender, prepare the yoghurt mixture and proceed as above.

*At a feast in Aghios Mamas on the slopes of Psiloreitis. Cretan women are cooking the traditional dish with goat in tomato sauce.*

# Goat
# in tomato sauce

1,5 kg meat, cut into serving pieces
1/2 cup oil
1 finely chopped onion
1 kilo tomatoes, finely chopped
salt, pepper

*A traditional autumn dish to be found all over Crete.*

Brown the meat and the onion in the oil, add 2 cups water and simmer for half an hour. Add the tomatoes, salt and pepper and some water, if needed.
Simmer till cooked.

# Liver
# in egg-lemon sauce

1 kilo lamb liver
4 tbsps olive oil
4 spring onions, finely chopped
2 heads lettuce, coarsely chopped
1 cup finely chopped dill
2 eggs, 2 lemons
salt, pepper

Put the liver into boiling salted water for 5 minutes. Take it out and chop it into small pieces.
Heat olive oil in a pot and sauté onions and liver for a few minutes. Add dill, salt, pepper and enough water to cover the liver. Simmer for 20 minutes, stir in lettuce and simmer for another half hour. Prepare the egg and lemon sauce: beat egg whites, add the yolks and then the lemon juice and a few spoonfuls of the stock beating constantly.
Remove the pot from the fire to keep the sauce from curdling, pour the mixture into the pot and stir.

*Pork with cellery*

## Pork with quinces

    1 kilo boneless pork
    1 kilo quinces
    1/2 cup olive oil
    3 grated tomatoes
    1 grated nutmeg
    salt and 1 tbsp sugar

Cut the meat in stewing pieces, wash and brown it in the olive oil on all sides. Add the tomatoes and 2 cups water and let the pork cook for about an hour, until almost tender.

Peel and core the quinces and cut in quarters. Salt and fry them lightly in 2 tbsps olive oil.

Add them immediately to the meat in the skillet. Sprinkle with the nutmeg and the sugar, pour in 1 cup water, if needed and simmer for another half hour.

*Picture of the dish on p. 56.*

## Pork with celery

    1 kilo boneless pork
    1,5 kilos celery, roughly chopped
    2 finely chopped onions
    1/2 cup olive oil
    the juice of 2 lemons
    salt and pepper

*This is the traditional dish served on the feast of Ayios Dimitrios in the village of Platanias, in Chania. All the housewives prepare pork with celery on the 26th of October, the nameday of the Saint. Saint Dimitrios is the patron saint of Platanias.*

Boil the celery in water for 5 minutes and drain.

Cut the meat into stewing pieces and brown it with the onions in the oil.

Add 2-3 cups water and let the pork cook for about three quarters of an hour. Add the celery, salt and pepper and continue cooking on low heat. Don't stir the food

*Pork with leeks*

with a spoon: simply gently shake the whole pot so as to avoid burning the meat. When the water has been absorbed and the meat is tender, add the lemon juice.

(Wild celery can also be used)

# Pork
# with leeks

    1 kilo boneless pork
    1,5 kilos leeks, coarsely chopped
    1/2 cup olive oil
    100 ml wine
    1/2 kilo grated tomatoes
    salt and pepper

Cut the meat into stewing pieces and wash it.

Heat the olive oil in a pot and brown the meat on all sides. Add the wine and 2 cups water and let the pork cook for about half an hour.

Add the leeks, the tomato, salt and pepper and continue cooking on low temperature, adding a little water, if needed.

# Pork soup
# with chondros
# (ground wheat)

    1 kilo pork meat, cut
    into serving pieces
    1 cup of "chondros" or
    "xinochondros" (see the
    "Pasta" chapter)
    2 eggs and 2 lemons
    salt

Place the meat in the pot, salt it, cover it with water, let it come to the boil and remove the froth on the surface. Then let it simmer until tender. When it has been cooked, take the meat out and strain the stock.

Clean the pot, add 2 more cups water and bring the stock to the boil; add the "chondros" or the "xinochondros" and the salt.

When the ground wheat is cooked (in 10-15 minutes), take the pot from the fire and prepare the egg and lemon sauce: beat the white and the yokes of the eggs separately, add the lemon juice.

Slowly add some of the stock, beating constantly. Finally pour the mixture into the pot stirring all the time and the soup is ready.

(This dish can also be cooked without the egg and lemon sauce).

# Pork
# wine snack

1 kg pork, cut into small cubes
6 tbsps olive oil
2 cloves of garlic, finely chopped
1/2 kilo chopped tomatoes
1/2 cup wine
salt, pepper, cumin

Brown the garlic lightly in the oil. Add the tomatoes and simmer for 15 minutes. Pour in the wine, salt, pepper, cumin and the meat. Simmer until tender.

# Grilled Pork

1 suckling pig
3-4 lemons cut into slices
1/2 cup olive oil
salt, pepper
oregano

Wash the piglet, cut it with a sharp knife but not entirely, put salt and lemon slices in the slits and let it stand for a few hours.

Baste the pig with the oil mixed with pepper and oregano and place it upside down in a large baking tin, upon vine or thyme twigs.

Roast at a low temperature for as long as it takes to get colour and become tender. Half way through, turn it over.

# Pork
# with potatoes

1 kilo pork meat
2 finely chopped onions
3 tbsps olive oil
1/2 cup finely chopped celery
1 bay leaf
1/2 kilo grated tomatoes
salt, pepper
1 kilo potatoes

Cut the meat into stewing pieces and brown it in a pot with the oil and the onion. Add the parsley, celery, laurel, tomatoes, salt, pepper and 4 cups water. Cover the pot and simmer for three quarters of an hour.

Meanwhile peel the potatoes, cut into quarters and place them in a baking tin. Add the cooked meat with its sauce on top of the potatoes and bake it in a moderate temperature for another 45 minutes.

*Rabbit with artichokes*

# Rabbit with artichokes

1 rabbit cut into serving portions
1 kilo potatoes cut into slices
1/2 kilo courgettes slit open on 2 sides
10 artichoke hearts halved
the juice of 2 lemons
salt, pepper
5-6 tbsps olive oil
and 1 cup olive oil for the frying

Prepare the artichokes: remove the outer leaves, trim the ends, rub with lemon juice and leave aside.
Put olive oil in a frying pan, heat and lightly fry the potatoes, the courgettes, the artichokes and finally the rabbit.
Transfer them all to a pot, add 5-6 tbsps olive oil, the lemon juice, 2 cups hot water, salt and pepper and simmer for 15 minutes.

# Rabbit stuffed with «myzithra»

1 medium sized rabbit
1 kilo "myzithra"
(See the "Cheeses" chapter)
2 tbsps olive oil
salt, pepper, oregano

Cover the rabbit with the spices and the olive oil and stuff it with the "myzithra". Then tie it up, or sew it with thread, wrap it up in grease proof paper and tie it again. Braise at a low temperature.

# Baked rabbit with yoghurt

1 rabbit cut into serving portions
2 lemons
1/2 cup olive oil
1/2 kilo yoghurt
4 eggs
salt, pepper

Wash the rabbit and marinade it for 3-4 hours

*Rabbit stew*

in the juice of the lemons. Then place it in a baking pan, add salt and pepper, pour the oil and 1/2 cup water over it and roast.

When cooked, take it out of the oven, mix the yoghurt with the beaten eggs and 2 or 3 tbsps of water and pour this mixture over the rabbit. Put the dish back into the oven until the yoghurt has set.

# Rabbit stew

1 medium sized rabbit
1/2 kilo roughly chopped onions
2 or 3 cloves of garlic
1/2 cup olive oil
100 ml red wine
1/2 kilo ripe tomatoes, finely chopped

half a tbsp of concentrated tomato pulp
2 cinnamon sticks
and 5 or 6 cloves
2 or 3 bay leaves
salt, pepper, cumin

Cut the rabbit into serving portions and brown it in the oil on all sides. Pour in the wine and let it simmer for 10 minutes. Then add the onions and when they are half cooked add the tomatoes and the tomato pulp diluted in a little water, the garlic, the bay leaves, the cinnamon, the cloves, salt and pepper, cumin and 1-2 cups water. Cook for about one more hour.

*Rabbit "xekafkaloto"*

# Rabbit "xekafkaloto"

1 small rabbit
olive oil for frying
1/2 cup flour
1 cup wine
salt, pepper

Cut the rabbit into serving portions and leave it to marinade in the wine for one hour.

Drain, add salt and pepper and brown the meat in hot oil on all sides. Then pour 100 ml wine and let it simmer for 15 more minutes.

(If the rabbit pieces aren't flat, beat them lightly before cooking).

# Hare in wine

1 medium-sized hare
1 cup red wine
2 or 3 onions, roughly chopped
2 cloves of garlic
3 or 4 bay leaves
2 or 3 cloves
salt, pepper
2 tbsps of flour
1/2 cup olive oil

Cut the hare into serving portions and marinade it overnight in the wine, the onions, the garlic, the bay leaves, the cloves and the pepper.

The next day brown it in the oil. Add the flour, stir and add the liquid in which the hare was marinating.

Add some salt and simmer till completely cooked.

*Chicken pilaff*

# Hare stew

1 medium-sized hare
1/2 cup olive oil
1 kilo onions
1/2 cup wine
1 tbsp concentrated
tomato pulp
3 or 4 bay leaves
salt, pepper
cumin
1 tbsp vinegar

Cut the hare into pieces and place in a pot with the oil, the salt and the wine. Let the mixture simmer for 15-20 minutes and then add the roughly chopped onions, the tomato pulp diluted in 1 cup water, the pepper, the cumin and the bay leaves. Simmer until meat is tender. Shortly before it has cooked, add the vinegar.

# Chicken and rice pilaff

1 medium sized chicken
2 cups rice
salt, juice of 1 lemon

Cut the chicken into large portions and place in a pot with salted water. Bring to the boil, skim the scum and let it cook until tender.
Take the meat out of the pot with a slotted spoon and place it on a dish. Measure out the stock, adding a little water so that you have 5 cups in all, bring back to the boil and add the rice. Boil for 10-15 minutes stirring a couple of times until almost all liquid has been absorbed and turn off the heat. Add the lemon juice to the pilaff, and if you like, a little "staka" (fresh goat's butter), stir and cover with a clean towel. Serve after 10 minutes.

*Chicken with dill*

## Chicken with dill

    1 medium-sized chicken
    1 kilo dill
    1/2 cup olive oil
    salt, pepper
    1 egg, 2 lemons

Wash the chicken and cut it into portions. Put it in a pot to brown in the oil and then add the dill. Pour in 2-3 cups of water, some salt and pepper: let it simmer.

When it has cooked, prepare the egg and lemon sauce: beat the egg, add the lemon, and some of the stock from the pot. Pour this mixture on the chicken, shake the pot to allow the egg-lemon sauce to combine with the food and remove the pot from the heat.

## Baked chicken with peas

    1 chicken
    1/2 cup olive oil
    the juice of 1 lemon
    1 kilo peas
    salt
    pepper

Cut the chicken into serving portions, salt them, place them in a baking pan with the skin underneath and pour the olive oil over them. Cover the pan with some sort of lid (today we can use aluminium foil) and place it in

*Baked chicken with peas*

the oven at a temperature of 200 degrees. Half an hour later uncover the pan, turn over the portions and baste them with lemon juice. Cook for 20 more minutes and add the peas, in between the meat. Pour in a little water if needed and cook for another half hour.

# Baked chicken with cheese

1 chicken
1/2 cheese, preferably "graviera" (gruyere)
2 tbsps olive oil
salt

Cut the chicken into serving portions and boil it in salty water until tender. Let it cool off and remove as many bones as you can.
Oil a pan, put the chicken pieces in the pan and place a slice of cheese ("graviera") on each piece.
Cook in the oven for 20-30 minutes, until the cheese melts.

# Chicken in the oven (pané)

1 chicken
2 cups bread crumbs
1 cup milk
salt, pepper

Cut the meat into portions. Salt and pepper each portion, dip it in milk, then in bread crumbs.
Place the pieces of chicken on a sheet of grease proof paper dabbed with olive oil and roast without turning the portions over.

# Chicken in tomato sauce

1 chicken
1/2 cup olive oil
1 onion, finely chopped
1 kilo ripe tomatoes
salt, pepper

Brown the chicken, cut in pieces, in the oil with the onion.
Then add the chopped tomatoes, salt, pepper and a little water. Simmer until tender.

# Chicken with okra

1 chicken
1/2 cup olive oil
1 kilo okra
1 finely chopped onion
1/2 cup lemon juice
1 kilo ripe tomatoes
salt, pepper

Brown the chicken in the oil with the onion and add the chopped tomatoes, salt, pepper and a little water.
When cooked, remove the chicken portions with a slotted spoon. In the meantime, prepare the okra: wash them, cut off the stems and pour half a cup of lemon juice or the juice of sour grapes ("agourida") over them. Let them stand for two or three hours before draining and adding them to the pot. Once cooked (after about 30-40 minutes), mix with the chicken.

# FISH

Fish was naturally to be found among the sea-side population of Crete, but was not at all common inland, especially in the most remote villages.

Rock fish, octopus and cuttlefish were among the favourites. "Kakavia" (a fish soup) was one of the most inexpensive and common dishes on the coast: it is made with a great variety of fish, boiled all together.

But other products, common to all Cretan households also had to be used: this inspired Cretan housewives and they concocted unusual dishes, mixing several different tastes.

Fish with okra is an example, a dish to be found in Sitia, Malia and the coastal villages of Rethymnon.

Preserved fish (salted cod -the Mediterranean version of cod-, dried cuttlefish or octopus) were quite common of old on Crete. Cretan housewives created many interesting recipes to include them in their cooking.

During long periods of religious fasting, fish is not consumed. Fish is only allowed to be eaten at big christian feasts which take place during the periods of fasting. Characteristic examples are 25th March, the Sunday before Easter Sunday and 6th August. On the eves of these celebrations, flotillas of boats go out to sea to try and satisfy the great demand for fish. Fish markets on Crete become especially busy on these days and there is a wide variety of fish available.

During the Lent period of the Orthodox Church, only sea food that has no blood is allowed, such as oysters and molluscs.

These are eaten in moderation and the way that they are prepared is of great gastronomical interest.

During Holy Week on Crete, you will be surprised by the amount of octopuses being cooked outside on grills.

Even in the traditional coffee houses of Heraklion, you can see octopuses hanging and being served as appetizers to accompany raki (the famous Cretan alcoholic drink).

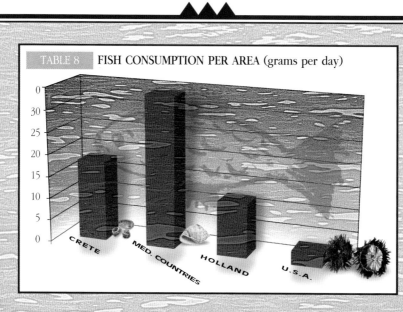

TABLE 8    FISH CONSUMPTION PER AREA (grams per day)

CRETE    MED. COUNTRIES    HOLLAND    U.S.A.

# FISH IN MODERATION!

Fish is not over consumed on Crete! Populations in other regions in the Mediterranean eat more fish than the inhabitants of Crete but these islanders consume more sea food than other European countries and the USA as is shown in the above table:

The latest dietary opinions agree with the consumption rate of fish on Crete.

The Cretans eat fish a few times a week, usually once or twice, depending on the distance of each area from the sea. As Serge Renaud notes, *"apart from having two fish meals a week, the fish eaters do not seem to have any added protection against disease... Research proves that one or two meals a week with fish merely help to maintain good health.*

*To double this fish intake would not help in protecting against the disastrous results which are incurred by sweets, fatty meat, butter, full fat milk and of course, smoking..."*

# FISH
# WITH VEGETABLES!

The main characteristic of cooking fish on Crete is the amazing combinations which can be achieved with a variety of vegetables and local seasonal greens! Not only do these produce harmonious flavours but also encourage good health.

The women of Crete are the ones to whom we now owe the survival of ancient recipes and along with their creativity; they have found ways of keeping the particular flavour of a certain fish, without smothering it in spices and rich sauces. In many cases, this helps the flavour of the fish.

The example of saupe fish is characteristic. It is a fish with a particular taste that is not liked by many.

These fish are usually caught in the summer when vegetables are at their best. Saupe is often cooked with okra. This sour vegetable does not disguise the taste of the fish but improves it to produce a much more mellow flavour!

# FISH SOUP - "Kakavia"

It is the most famous and common dish of the fishermen on the Greek islands. It is both a delicious and wholesome dish, particularly popular among the people of the coastal regions of Crete. At Mochlos, the picturesque sea-side settlement of the province of Sitia, fish soup was the food cooked on Whit Monday. On that day the people of the nearby villages went down to the seaside and celebrated all together with good wine and violins or lyres. They often cooked plenty of fish soup in big dixies, using the best fish caught by the fishermen on that day.

In many coastal villages of Crete, where Saint Nikolaos, protector of the seamen, is worshipped as their patron saint, fish soup is the main dish on 6th December, the day of the saint's feast.

At Aghios Nikolaos, the beautiful tourist town of Eastern Crete, the fishermen used to offer people fish soup on 6th December each year.

On Crete, apart from the usual fish used in the preparation of "kakavia", red mullet is also used. One could say that "kakavia is the official and exceptional fish dish cooked in most areas of Crete.

It seems that "kakavia" is an evolution of an ancient Greek dish which was cooked in a special pot, the "kakavi" (cauldron). This is where the name "kakavia" is derived from...

**Ingredients:**
1,5 kg of big fish
(red snapper, grouper, sea bass, cod, pike etc.)
1/2 kilo small fish (gurnard, scorpion fish etc.)
1 or 2 tomatoes
a bunch of parsley
a bunch of celery
2 onions
4 tbsps olive oil
salt, pepper
the juice of 2 lemons

Scrape, wash and gut the fish. Cut into thick slices, sprinkle with salt and a little lemon juice and leave aside.

Put enough water in a large pot, bring it to the boil and add the oil, the tomatoes and the onion sliced open, the parsley, the celery roughly chopped, salt and pepper.

After this has been cooking for 10 minutes, put in the smaller fish and cook until they dissolve.

Strain the soup and add the big fish to the pot: cook for about a quarter of an hour. Finally, add the lemon juice.

# Poached fish - fish soup with vegetables

1 or 2 large fish (sea-bream, dentex, grouper, gurnard (piper), blackfish etc.)
2 or 3 onions
2 tomatoes
a bunch of celery
5 or 6 carrots
1/2 kilo courgettes
1/2 kilo potatoes
4 tbsps olive oil
1/2 cup rice
2 eggs, 2 lemons
salt and pepper

Scrape, wash and gut the fish. Cut into thick slices, sprinkle with salt and a little lemon juice and leave aside.

Put plenty of water in a large pot, bring to the boil and add the potatoes and the carrots cut in pieces, the courgettes, the tomatoes and the onions sliced open, the celery roughly chopped and finally the olive oil and salt. When the vegetables are half cooked, add the fish. Once the fish is cooked, in about 15 minutes, take all the ingredients out carefully with a slotted spoon and place them in a large dish with the fish in the middle and the different vegetables all around it.

Now strain the fish stock and return to the pot; when it comes to the boil again, put in the rice and let it cook for 10-15 minutes before taking the pot off the heat.

The soup can be served simply with lemon, or with an egg and lemon sauce; beat the eggs, add the lemon juice and finally, slowly add a few ladlefuls from the soup, stirring constantly.

Pour the sauce back into the pot and stir: the soup is ready.

(You can blend some of the vegetables and add them to the stock).

# Fish soup ("Kakavia") of the Libyan Sea

1 kilo big fish
(e. g. sea bass, red snapper)
1/2 kilo potatoes cut into slices
2 medium onions cut into slices

*Fish with okra*

2-3 courgettes sliced open
(optional)
4-5 tbsps olive oil
salt, pepper
the juice of 2 lemons or
1 teaspoon citric acid

Scrape, wash and gut the fish. Cut into thick slices.
Place the ingredients in a large pot in layers, first the onion, then the potatoes and finally the fish. Add salt and pepper, drizzle with olive oil, cover with water, put the lid on the pot and cook the fish on a high temperature for 15-20 minutes. Uncover the pot, pour in the lemon juice or the citric acid and turn off the heat.

# Swordfish on the spit

1 kilo sword fish
2 firm tomatoes
2 green peppers
2 onions
1/2 cup olive oil
juice of 1 lemon
salt, pepper

Clean both fish and vegetables and cut into cubes. Marinate them in a mixture made with the olive oil, the lemon juice, salt and pepper.
Skewer the cubes alternatively. Grill gently.

# Monkfish on the spit

The same as above (swordfish on the spit).

# Fish with okra

1 kilo fish (preferably sea-bass, red snapper or saupe)
1 kilo okra
1/2 cup olive oil
1/2 kilo tomatoes
1 or 2 onions
1/2 cup lemon juice or vinegar
salt, pepper

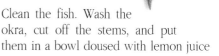

Clean the fish. Wash the okra, cut off the stems, and put them in a bowl doused with lemon juice

*Baked fish with courgettes*

or vinegar. Leave in the sun for 2-3 hours (this is so they won't dissolve in the cooking).

Brown the onion in a pot and add the okra, the tomatoes, salt, pepper and 1-2 cups water and simmer till half cooked. Remove half the okra, place the fish on the okra in the pot and add the other half. Cook for another 20 minutes without stirring the food; only shake the pot from time to time to prevent the food from sticking.

(This dish can also be cooked in the oven).

# Baked fish with courgettes

1 kilo big fish
(preferably filleted fish)
1 kilo courgettes
1/2 kilo tomatoes
1/2 cup olive oil
1 finely chopped onion
salt, pepper

Wash, slice open and salt the courgettes. Clean and salt the fish and place it in the middle of an oiled baking pan.

Lightly fry the courgettes and place them all around the fish.

In the same oil, brown the onion, add the crushed tomatoes and cook the sauce for 10 minutes. Pour this sauce over the fish and the courgettes.

Add pepper, a little water and bake in a moderate oven for about an hour.

*Tuna fish in tomato sauce*

# Fish stew

1 kilo big fish
(preferably sea bass, dentex or monkfish)
4-5 roughly chopped onions
2 cloves of garlic, finely chopped
1/2 cup olive oil
1/2 kilo crushed tomatoes or
1 tbsp concentrate pulp
3-4 tbsps wine
1 cinnamon stick
salt, pepper

Scrape, wash and gut the fish. Cut into thick slices, sprinkle with salt and a little lemon juice and leave aside.
Heat the olive oil in a pan and brown the onion and the garlic. Stir in wine, tomato, cinnamon stick, salt, pepper and 1-2 cups water and simmer for 15 minutes.
Add the fish and cook for 20 more minutes.

# Tuna fish in tomato sauce

1 kilo fresh tuna fish
1 cup vinegar
1/2 cup olive oil
2 finely chopped onions
1 or 2 cloves garlic, finely chopped
4 or 5 ripe tomatoes, finely chopped
salt, pepper

Cut the fish into slices and wash it. (If you like, you can bleach it first in a cup of vinegar for one hour).
Brown the onion and the garlic in the oil, then add the tuna slices turning them over several times.
Pour in the tomatoes and a cup of water, salt and pepper; let the tuna simmer in this sauce for about half an hour.

# Parrot fish in tomato sauce

1 kilo parrot fish
4 tbsps olive oil and olive oil for frying
the juice of 1 lemon
1/2 kilo finely chopped tomatoes
1 finely chopped onion
4 tbsps white wine
salt, pepper

Wash the fish and remove the guts (although you can leave them on. You must, however, remove the gal). Baste with lemon juice and salt, then leave them aside for one hour.

Dredge parrot fish lightly in flour and fry in hot olive oil on both sides. Place on kitchen roll until you prepare the **sauce:** heat 4 tbsps olive oil in a skillet and brown the onion. Add tomato, wine, salt and pepper and simmer until the sauce thickens. Pour the sauce over the fish and serve either hot or cold.

*Sea bass with purslane*

## Sea bass with purslane

1 kilo sea bass
1 finely chopped onion
1 clove of finely chopped garlic
1/2 kilo crushed tomatoes
1 kilo roughly chopped purslane
salt, pepper

Scrape, wash and gut the fish. Cut into slices and sauté in the oil, turning them over to brown evenly. Take the fish out and put the onion in the skillet. Brown the onion for a few minutes and add the garlic, the tomato, the purslane and 1 cup water. Cook for 10 minutes and place the fish again in the skillet, over the purslane. Salt and pepper. Cook for another 10 minutes.

## Baked fish with potatoes

1 kilo fish (sliced or whole)
1/2 cup olive oil
1/2 kilo tomatoes

a bunch of parsley
2 cloves of garlic
1/2 cup bread crumbs
salt, pepper
the juice of one lemon

Scrape, wash and gut the fish.
Finely chop the parsley and the garlic and mix with salt, pepper and bread crumbs. Chop the tomatoes and place half of them in a baking pan.
Place the fish on top and sprinkle with the above mixture of parsley, garlic and so on. Then add the rest of the tomatoes, drizzle the whole dish with the oil and lemon juice and cook in the oven for about an hour.

## Baked fish with oil and oregano

1 kilo fish (either big or smaller ones, like pilchard or sardines)
1 kilo potatoes
1/2 cup olive oil
the juice of 2 lemons
salt, pepper
2 tbsps oregano

Clean and gut the fish and, if it's big, cut it into slices.

Place it in the middle of an oiled pan with the sliced potatoes all around it. Sprinkle with salt, pepper and oregano. Drizzle with the oil, the lemon juice and a little water and cook it in the oven in moderate heat for about an hour.

# Poached sardines

Wash and gut sardines and boil them in salty water for 10-15 minutes.
Serve with olive oil and lemon juice.

# Baked pilchard with tomatoes

> 1 kilo pilchard
> 5-6 tbsps olive oil
> 1 cup finely chopped parsley
> 3-4 grated tomatoes
> 1 grated onion
> salt, pepper

Wash and gut the fish. Salt and pepper and place in oiled baking pan. Mix remaining olive oil with tomato, onion and parsley and sprinkle over the fish. Bake at high temperature for 20 minutes and then continue at medium temperature for another 30 minutes.

# Baked fish with green peppers

## Fried red mullet

> 1 kilo red mullet
> juice of 2 lemons
> salt
> olive oil and flour for frying

A common dish on the islands and the coast of Crete. Instead of red mullet, one can use other fish (smelt, fresh sardine, bream, sole etc.).

Scrape, wash and gut the fish. Douse with the lemon juice and salt and leave aside for an hour or two.

Dredge the fish with flour and deep-fry in olive oil until both sides are golden brown. Serve in a large dish garnished with some parsley.

Lemon juice is to be used sparingly as it softens the light crust obtained through frying the fish.

## Red bream or red mullet on the grill

> 1 kilo of large sized fish
> (5 to 6 fish for a kilo)
> 1/2 cup olive oil
> 2 lemons
> a small bunch of finely chopped parsley
> salt

Clean, wash and gut the fish. Baste them with olive oil and salt and place them on the grill. Let them brown gently, turning and basting them with oil at regular intervals.

Serve in a large dish with slices of lemon and parsley.

Prepare some oil and lemon sauce which you can pour on the fish or serve

> 1 kilo fish (preferably monkfish or red snapper)
> 1 kilo green peppers
> 1/2 cup olive oil
> salt, pepper

Clean and gut the fish and cut it into slices.

Cut the green peppers in round slices and place half of them in a baking pan.

On top, put the fish sprinkled with salt and pepper and over it, the rest of the green peppers.

Pour on the oil and cook in a moderate oven for about an hour.

# Red mullet with artichokes

1 kilo artichoke hearts
1 kilo red mulllet
1 finely chopped onion
1/2 cup olive oil
the juice of 2 lemons
salt, pepper

Scrape, wash and gut the fish. Prepare the artichokes: remove the outer leaves and trim the ends, rub with lemon juice and leave aside.

Heat olive oil in a skillet, brown the onion and add the artichokes with the lemon juice, salt, pepper and 1 cup hot water.

Cook the artichokes for quarter of an hour and then place the fish on top of them. Cook for another 10 minutes.

*Porgy on the grill*

separately so that it can be added individually.

Fishermen, however, prefer eating fish which have a strong taste, as is the case of the red mullet, without parsley or oregano, or any other trimmings.

# Porgy on the grill

This fish has more fat than red mullet, therefore grill it using less olive oil for basting.

# Grouper aspic

1,5-2 kilos grouper
1 onion sliced open
the juice of 1 lemon and
1 bitter orange
salt, pepper
cummin

Scrape, wash and gut the fish. Put it in a large pot with the onion. More than cover with water and boil the fish for about 20 minutes.

Remove the fish from the pot and, when it cools off, debone it.

Strain 3 cups of fish stock, add the juice, salt, pepper and cumin.

Place the fish back in the liquid: bring to the boil.

Once it has cooked, place it in a large bowl and leave to set.

# Fried picarel - fried atherine (silverside)

Small fish are usually fried in hot oil. If the fish is tiny, don't try cleaning it: simply roll it in flour and deep-fry.

In the Cretan villages on the coast, the tiny fish are often bunched up by their tails after rolling them in flour (flour helps keep them together); they are then all fried in groups and are easier to serve.

*Fried picarel and atherine*

# Cuttlefish in wine

   1 kilo cuttlefish
   1/2 cup olive oil
   1-2 roughly chopped onions
   1/2 cup dry white wine
   salt, pepper

Clean the cuttlefish: remove the eyes, the single bone, the stomach and the ink. Rinse well and cut into strips.
Brown the onion in the oil and add the cuttlefish. Cook for 15-20 minutes, stirring occasionally, until all liquid has been absorbed. Pour in the wine, a cup of water, salt and pepper and simmer until most liquid has been absorbed and cuttlefish is tender.

# Cuttlefish in ink sauce

As above, with the only difference that, along with the wine, you add the ink of 2-3 cuttlefish diluted in 1 cup water.

# Cuttlefish with spinach

   1 kilo cuttlefish
   1 kilo spinach
   1/2 cup olive oil
   2 finely chopped onions
   1/2 cup white wine
   1 bunch dill or fennel,
   finely chopped
   1 bunch of mint, finely chopped
   salt, pepper

Wash and roughly chop the spinach.
Clean, rinse and cut the cuttlefish into strips.
Heat olive oil in a skillet, brown the onion and add dill or fennel, mint and the cuttlefish.
Sauté for 15 minutes until most liquid has been absorbed and stir in wine, salt, pepper and 1-2 cups water; simmer until cuttlefish is soft.
Add spinach and cook for 10 more minutes.

# Cuttlefish stew

1 kilo cuttlefish
1/2 cup olive oil
1 kilo onions
4 tbsps vinegar
1 tbsp concentrated tomato pulp
or 1/2 kilo finely chopped tomatoes
2 or 3 bay leaves
salt, pepper

Clean, rinse and cut the cuttlefish into strips.
Brown the onions in the oil. Add the cuttlefish and cook on a low temperature for half an hour adding 1 cup of water.
Add vinegar, tomato pulp diluted in 1 cup water, the bay leaves, pepper, and a little salt and cook for another half hour.

# Cuttlefish and rice pilaff

1 kilo cuttlefish
1/2 cup olive oil
2 onions, finely chopped
1 tbsp concentrated tomato pulp
or 1/2 kilo finely chopped tomatoes
1/2 kilo rice
salt, pepper

Clean, rinse and cut the cuttlefish into pieces.
Brown the onions in the oil and add the cuttlefish. Let them cook a few minutes until all liquid has been absorbed.
Stir in the tomatoes, pepper and salt and simmer for about an hour. Add more water to the pot so that you have 6 cups of liquid in all and return to the boil.
Add the rice and stir at intervals for about 15 minutes until liquid has been absorbed.

# Cuttlefish with "kritharaki" (barley-shaped pasta)

As before, (cuttlefish with rice).

# Cuttlefish with potatoes

1 kilo cuttlefish
1/2 cup olive oil
2 onions, finely chopped
1/2 kilo finely chopped tomatoes
1 kilo potatoes in slices
salt, pepper

Clean, rinse and cut the cuttlefish into pieces.
Brown the onions in the oil and add the cuttlefish. Let them cook a few minutes until all liquid has been absorbed. Stir in the tomato, pepper and salt and simmer for about half an hour. Add the potatoes, 2 cups water and a little salt and simmer without stirring the food; only shake the pot at intervals to prevent the food from sticking to the bottom of the pot.

# Octopus with rice

See cuttlefish with rice.

# Octopus in vinegar

1 kilo octopus
1/2 cup olive oil
2 or 3 cloves of garlic
4-5 tbsps vinegar
pepper, oregano

Wash the octopus and remove the ink sac and mouth. Put it in a pot and cook on low heat without adding any water.

Only add water if it has absorbed its own and isn't yet completely cooked. Then remove it from the heat and cut it up in small pieces.

Beat the vinegar with the oil, the finely chopped garlic, the pepper and the oregano and pour this over the octopus. (Octopus doesn't need any salt).

# Octopus in wine

1 kilo octopus
1/2 cup olive oil
1/2 cup red wine
pepper

Wash the octopus and remove the ink sac and mouth. Cut it into small pieces. Heat olive oil in a pot, add octopus and let it cook on low heat until all liquid has been absorbed.

Pour in the wine, let it simmer, add pepper. Simmer until the octopus is soft, adding some water, if necessary.

# Octopus stew

See cuttlefish stew.

# Octopus with short macaroni

1 kilo octopus
1/2 kilo short macaroni
1/2 cup olive oil
1 finely chopped onion
1/2 kilo grated tomatoes
100 ml red wine
salt and pepper

Wash the octopus and remove the ink sac and mouth. Cut it into small pieces.

Brown the onion in the oil and add the octopus. Let it cook, absorbing its own water. Pour in the wine, and let it simmer. Then, add the tomato, salt and pepper and 1 cup water; simmer until it is soft.

Remove the octopus from the pot, pour in 6 cups water and when it comes to the boil again, add the macaroni. Serve the octopus with the pasta in the same dish.

# Octopus on the grill

Wash the octopus and remove the ink sac and mouth. Put it in a pot and cook over low heat without adding any water.

Take it out of the pot, brush with olive oil mixed with pepper and grill it for 10-15 minutes, turning it a few times to cook evenly.

Once cooked, cut into chunks and serve doused with olive oil and vinegar or lemon juice and seasoned with oregano.

# Octopus balls

1 kilo octopus
2 thick slices of stale bread, soaked in wine and squeezed lightly
2 eggs, slightly beaten
1/2 cup finely chopped parsley

1 teasp oregano
2 grated onions
pepper
flour and olive oil for frying

Wash the octopus and remove the ink sac and mouth. Put it in a pot with enough water and boil it for 5 minutes.

Remove from the pot and, when it cools off a little, place it in the deep freeze for a couple of hours. When it is frozen, mince it. Add the above ingredients and knead to combine them well (although, according to fishermen, the parsley may impair the taste of the octopus). Shape the balls, dredge with flour and deep fry in olive oil. Serve with a good strong white wine.

# Tuna fish balls

The same as above, having frozen the tuna fish so as to mince it.

# Fried squid

Clean and wash the squid, removing the eyes, the mouth, the jelly-like strip from the back, the ink and the innards.

Separate the tentacles from the stomach; leave the tentacles whole and cut the stomach into round slices.

Season with salt and pepper, dredge with flour and deep-fry in ample olive oil. Serve hot, sprinkled with lemon juice.

# Squid
# in tomato sauce

1 kilo squid
1/2 cup olive oil
1 or 2 finely chopped onions
a small bunch of parsley
1/2 kilo tomatoes
salt, pepper

Wash and clean the squid as above and cut into pieces.
Brown the onion in the oil and add the squid. Sauté for 10 minutes and add the grated tomatoes, the chopped parsley, salt and pepper. Let this cook until the sauce thickens.

## SALTED COD

*Long ago, salted cod was one of the most common products of the fishing industry of Crete, and, naturally, it was to be found most often in the regions that were farthest from the sea. The price was accessible to everybody, hence its name of "ftocho-yiannis", which means: poor John, thereby implying that it is a dish of the poor. It was prepared in many different ways, with all the other products of the Cretan land: with pulses, greens, cereals...*

# Salted cod
# in lemon-flour sauce

800 grams of salted cod
1/2 cup olive oil
1 grated onion
1/2 kilo potatoes
1/2 cup
finely chopped dill
1/2 cup finely chopped parsley
pepper
2 or 3 tbsps flour
the juice of 2 lemons

Desalt the cod the night before: cut the cod into slices and place in a large basin with plenty of water. Soak the cod for at least 15 hours changing the water a couple of times.
Brown the onion in the oil in a pot. Add 2 cups of water, bring to the boil and add the dill, the parsley, the potatoes, cut into pieces and simmer. Then, carefully add the slices of cod and the pepper and cook for another 20 minutes.
Dissolve the flour in a little warm water, add the lemon juice: mix this with the food in the pot. Bring to the boil and remove from the fire: the dish is ready.

# Fried salted cod

800 grams of salted cod
1 cup flour
1 cup water
1 egg
a little salt

Desalt the cod cut in slices by leaving it in water the day before and changing the water 3-4 times.

Make a batter with the water, the flour, the egg and a little salt.

Dip the cod slices, one by one, in this batter and fry them in hot oil.

# Baked salted cod with potatoes

1 fillet of salted cod
1 kilo potatoes
2 finely chopped onions
2 or 3 cloves of garlic,
finely chopped
1/2 kilo grated tomatoes
1/2 cup olive oil
1 tbsp oregano
1 cup finely chopped parsley
salt, pepper

Desalt the cod cut in slices, leaving it in water from the day before and changing the water 3-4 times.

Slice the potatoes and place them in a baking pan.

Season with salt, pepper, parsley and oregano. Then place the fish, sprinkling it with oregano, pepper and garlic; finally, repeat the first step with the potatoes.

Pour the tomatoes and the oil over the whole dish and bake.

# Salted cod stew with potatoes

1 kilo salted cod
1/2 cup olive oil
2 onions
1/2 kilo tomatoes
a small bunch of finely
chopped parsley
1 kilo potatoes cut into
quarters
salt
pepper

Desalt the cod the night before: cut the cod into slices and place in a large basin with plenty of water. Soak the cod for at least 15 hours, changing the water a couple of times.

Brown the finely chopped onions in the oil and add the crushed tomatoes, the parsley, the salt and pepper. Let this cook for 5 minutes and add the potatoes; simmer for 20 minutes, add the desalted cod and cook for another quarter of an hour or so.

# Cod with celery

1 kilo cod
(either fresh or salted)
1 kilo celery
1/2 cup olive oil
1 finely chopped onion
the juice of 2 lemons
1 tbsp flour
salt
pepper

Clean and gut the cod if it is fresh, otherwise, desalt it the night before: cut into slices and place in a large bowl with plenty of water. Soak the cod for at least 15 hours changing the water a couple of times.

Wash celery, chop it roughly and boil in water for 5 minutes. Drain.

In a large skillet heat olive oil and brown the onion. Add celery, salt, pepper and enough water to cover it. Simmer for 50 minutes or so. Place the cod on top of the celery, cook for 15 minutes and turn the cod slices to cook on the other side for a further 15 minutes.

Dissolve flour in the lemon juice, add more liquid from the pot and empty all the mixture over the food. Cook for 5 minutes before removing the pot from the heat.

# Salted cod with chickpeas

700 grams salted cod
300 grams chickpeas
1/2 cup olive oil
1 finely chopped onion
1/2 kilo grated tomatoes
salt, pepper

Put cod and chickpeas together in a large bowl with water the day before. Change the water a couple of times and the next day take the cod slices out of the bowl and strain the chickpeas.

Heat olive oil in a skillet and brown the onion. Add the chickpeas, pepper and the tomatoes. Cover with water and simmer for an hour or so. Place cod slices on top of the chickpeas and cook for another 20-30 minutes. Add a little salt, if needed.

and sauté for a few minutes, stirring with a wooden spoon. Beat the eggs together with 3 tbsps liquid from the pot, a little salt and pepper. Pour the eggs over the shrimps, cook for 5 minutes and carefully flip the omelet and cook for another 5 minutes until that side is golden brown, too.

# Crab pilaff

2-3 crabs
2 cups rice
salt, pepper
3 tbsps olive oil

Wash and boil the crabs for 20 minutes. Strain them. Detach the limbs and pound them.

# Shrimp omelette

1/2 kilo shrimps
3 tbsps olive oil
4 eggs
salt, pepper

Clean and wash shrimps and boil them for 5-10 minutes in ample salted water. Rinse them well, drain and remove shells and heads. Heat olive oil in a frying pan, add shrimps

*Crab pilaff*

Place them in a colander, pour water over them and mix the liquid with the water in which you boiled the crabs.
Measure out the liquid (you need 5 cups), put it in the pot again, bring to the boil and stir in the rice. Add salt and pepper and cook for about 15 minutes, stirring from time to time.
Finally, heat the olive oil and pour it over the pilaff.

# Sea-urchin salad

20-25 sea urchins
2 tbsps olive oil
2 tbsps lemon juice

Only the female urchins, those with a reddish-purple colour are edible. You can collect them yourself as they cluster together on rocks.
With a sharp knife or pointed scissors remove the soft side carefully with a circular motion.
Rinse each urchin well (preferably with sea water) discarding the digestive system and leaving the coral intact.
Detach the coral from the sides of the shells and place in a bowl.
Serve drizzled with olive oil and lemon juice.

# SNAILS

A Cretan speciality! Cretans love them and prepare them in more than 40 ways, creating delicious dishes. The combinations with chondros (ground wheat) or with vegetables are among the most famous, but the most popular dish is "snails boubouristi".

Cretan cuisine is the richest and most inventive in the preparation of snail dishes. It employs the products available in each season.

In Spring, snails are wonderfully combined with vegetables, fennel leaves, fresh broad beans, wild greens...

In Summer, with courgettes, okra, aubergines.

All year round, with spinach, and so on...

## AGAINST HEART DISEASES!

Recent studies have shown that Cretan snails, fed with a great variety of greens and herbs, contain significant amounts of α-linolenic acid, which reduces the risk of heart diseases considerably.

However, this is not true with all snails, especially those grown in organized production units, which are not fed with wild greens and herbs.

## HISTORICAL REVIEW

A common dish in Minoan Crete, especially in the countryside: Minoan archaeological finds gave light to a vessel full of snails on the island of Santorini. It was a food easy to find, free of the toil and uncertainty of hunting... In ancient Greece it was the poor man's meal: snails were abundant and free.

Nevertheless, those who were well-off also liked snails, "kochli" as they were known, or "chochli" as they are still called on Crete, where they've kept their ancient name. As Galen (5, 669) tells us: "*All Greeks eat them*".

During the Byzantine years, snails continued to be a favourite dish all over the Greek world, especially on Crete where then, as now, they were eaten with rice or ground wheat.

To this day, snails are cooked throughout the year, after having been kept in clean sacks of a loose fabric, which lets the air in. But if they remain in the sacks too long, they become thinner and lose their taste.

It is said that Cretan snails, especially those to be found in the mountains and in uncultivated areas, are the best.

This is because the flora of the island is made of many aromatic herbs, which are the best food for snails and give them this wonderfully individual taste. According to the season, one can employ a dozen different ways of cooking snails on Crete.

# The preparation of the snails

Snails are gathered and put away in loosely knit sacks, until they're to be cooked. One must remember that they're alive and therefore they may die, for a number of reasons: a single dead one will ruin the enjoyment of a dish of snails because of the bad smell it exudes.

Snails must be carefully cleaned and the membrane covering the orifice must be removed: the larger the membrane, the larger and juicier the snail.

Put them in water for a little while and you will immediately see them come back to life: one by one, they come out of their shells, making it easy to see if, by chance, there are any dead ones. With a pin try to get those that don't come out of their shells to react and, if they don't, discard them.

In every case, let the snails boil in salted water until you can remove the froth (which is in fact their saliva).

Then, clean them one by one, with a small knife, scraping away any debris or bits of the membrane that may still be around the orifice or on the shell.

Rinse well and the snails are ready to be cooked...

# Boiled snails

1/2 kilo snails
2 or 3 bay leaves
5 or 6 peppercorns
1/2 cup vinegar
salt, lemon juice

*Boiled snails are the most common dish during Lent, and especially during Holy Week, when oil consumption is also forbidden.*
*An excellent "meze" (snack) to accompany raki or "tsikoudia", the popular alcoholic drink of Crete.*

The snails are cleaned with the utmost care (see above) and put in a pot, covered in water which is brought to the boil: the stum, which is nothing more than their saliva, can thus be removed.
Change the water, add the salt, the vinegar, the bay leaves and the peppercorns, bring back to the boil and add the snails.
Let them boil for 10 minutes and serve with vinegar or lemon juice.

# Boiled snails
## with oil and lemon juice or with oil and vinegar

As above.
Before serving, pour either oil and lemon juice or oil and vinegar over them.

# Shepherd's snails

1 kilo snails
1/2 cup olive oil
1 tbsp flour
the juice of 2 lemons

Prepare the snails as above.
Put them back in the pot with the oil, the lemon juice and the flour. Boil for 5 more minutes and then serve.

# Snails "boubouristi"

1/2 kilo large snails
1/2 olive oil for frying
salt
3-4 tbsps vinegar
1 tbsp rosemary

*This is the most common way of preparing snails on Crete, especially when a group of friends gets together. It is an excellent "meze" for wine but also an equally appreciated snack for "tsikoudia".*

Prepare the snails as above.
Spread a thin layer of salt (2-3 teaspoons) in a frying pan and place the snails upon it in a single layer, open side down.
After 5 minutes add olive oil and cook for another 10 minutes, stirring occasionally. Pour in vinegar and rosemary and serve them together with the juice of the pan.

*Right: Shepherd's snails*

# Snails with fennel and potatoes

1/2 kilo snails
1 kilo finely chopped fennel
1 kilo potatoes cut into slices
1/2 cup olive oil
salt, pepper
the juice of 1 lemon

Prepare the snails as above.
In a saucepan heat olive oil and sauté fennel for 5 minutes. Cover with water and simmer for half an hour. Add potatoes and a cup of water. Cook for 15 minutes and add snails, salt, pepper and lemon juice.
Simmer for another 15 minutes, until almost all liquid has been absorbed.

# Snails with artichokes and fresh broad beans

1/2 kilo snails
1 kilo green broad beans
1/2 kilo artichoke hearts
1/2 cup olive oil
1 cup finely chopped dill
or fennel
2 tbsps vinegar
1 tbsp flour
2-3 fresh garlic leaves,
finely chopped
salt, pepper

Prepare the snails as above.
Prepare the artichokes: cut off the outer leaves and trim the ends, rub with lemon juice and leave aside.
Prepare the broad beans: if they are very tender, keep both the broad beans and the pods cutting off the edges and the fibres from both sides. If they are too big, discard the pods.
Heat olive oil in a saucepan and sauté garlic and dill or fennel for 10 minutes. Add snails, broad beans and 1 cup water and simmer for quarter of an hour. Add artichokes, salt, pepper and cover with water.
Simmer and when almost done, take a little liquid from the pot to mix the flour and the vinegar before returning all this to the pot. Shake the pot to mix well. Bring to the boil and serve.

# "Sympetherio" with snails, aubergines and "xinochondros"

1/2 kilo snails
1/2 cup olive oil
1 finely chopped
onion

*Snails with "chondros"*

1 kilo aubergines
1 cup "xinochondros"
(see the chapter on Pasta)
1/2 kilo grated tomatoes
salt and pepper

Cut the aubergines in small pieces, salt them and let them stand for one hour.
Prepare the snails as above.
Rinse the aubergines, drain and sauté for a few minutes in a saucepan with the oil and the onion.
Add snails and the tomatoes and simmer for 10 minutes.

Pour in 2-3 cups water, bring to the boil and stir in the "xinochondros", some salt and pepper. Simmer and stir regularly for 15-20 minutes, until cooked.

# Snails with "chondros"

1/2 kilo snails
1/2 kilo
"chondros"
(ground wheat)
1/2 cup olive oil
2 grated onions
2 grated courgettes
4 ripe grated
tomatoes
salt, pepper

Prepare the snails as above.
Heat olive oil in a pot and add onions, courgettes, snails and the tomatoes. Sauté for 5 minutes and pour in 2 cups water, salt and pepper; simmer for half an hour.
Remove the snails from the pot and put them aside.
Add 5-6 cups water to the remaining sauce, bring to the boil and stir in the "chondros" and a little salt.

Simmer for 20 minutes stirring often to keep the "chondros" from sticking to the bottom of the pot.

Once the "chondros" has been cooked and has absorbed most of the liquid, return the snails to the pot, give a good stir and remove the pot from the heat.

# Snails
# and rice pilaff

1/2 kilo snails
2 cups rice
1/2 cup olive oil
1 finely chopped onion
3 large ripe grated tomatoes
salt, pepper

Prepare the snails as above.
Brown the finely chopped onion in a pot with the oil.
Add the snails and, after a few minutes, the tomatoes, salt, pepper and 1-2 cups water.
Cook for 10 minutes, then remove the snails from the pot, add more water (about 5-6 cups), bring to the boil again and then add the rice.
When the rice is half-cooked, return the snails to the pot.
Simmer for a few minutes, stirring constantly and the dish is ready.

# Holy Thursday
# snails

1/2 kilo snails
1 kilo courgettes
1 kilo artichoke hearts
1 kilo potatoes
olive oil for frying
2 or 3 lemons
salt
pepper

*On Holy Thursday, as opposed to the day before and the day after, olive oil is not forbidden. This dish was very common in the region of Messara, where, even before the advent of green-houses, courgettes were to be found in early spring.*

Prepare the snails as above.
Prepare the artichokes: cut off the outer leaves and trim the ends, rub with lemon juice and leave aside.
Cut the potatoes into large slices and fry them lightly in a pan, just enough to colour them, not to cook them.
Slit open the courgettes and the artichokes and fry them, like the potatoes, in the pan. Add the snails to the pan for a few minutes.
Now put all the ingredients in a large pot, including the frying oil, which is still hot, salt pepper, lemon juice and 2 cups hot water.
Cook for 10-15 minutes.

*Snails and rice pilaff*

*Snails with courgettes and garlic*

# Snails with courgettes and garlic

1/2 kilo large snails
1 kilo courgettes
1/2 kilo potatoes
2 finely chopped onions
1/2 cup olive oil
1/2 kilo finely chopped tomatoes
5 or 6 cloves of garlic,
finely chopped
salt, pepper

*A favourite summer dish all over the island.*

Prepare the snails as above.
Brown the onions in the oil and add the snails, the tomatoes, salt and pepper. Simmer for 10 minutes before adding 3 cups water, the garlic, the potatoes cut into slices and the courgettes, slit open (that is, they're cut in four, but not all the way through, so as to remain in one piece). Simmer on a low heat until most liquid has been absorbed.

# Snail stew

1/2 kilo large snails
1/2 kilo onions
1/2 cup olive oil
1/2 kilo tomatoes
or 1 tbsp of concentrated tomato pulp
5 or 6 bay leaves
1/2 cup red wine
salt, pepper

Prepare the snails as above.
Brown the onions and add the snails. Sauté them for 5 minutes stirring a couple of times and add chopped tomatoes, salt and pepper.
Bring to the boil before adding the wine and the bay leaves. Pour in 1 cup water and simmer until the sauce thickens.

# FRUIT - GREENS - VEGETABLES
## ANTIOXIDANTS AT THE TABLE!

Cretans consume large quantities of fruit, greens and vegetables! Never a day goes by without one of these products being a part of a meal.

The island produces large amounts of oranges and mandarines. Water and honey melons are cultivated, but to a lesser extent, as well as pears, peaches and apricots. Apples from the Lassithi Plateau and cherries from Amari and Milopotamo are well known throughout the island.

During the summer months, an abundance of figs and even more grapes are consumed. There are vines throughout the island which produce a large variety of both grapes to be eaten and those to be pressed to make wine. Whilst in season, many fruit are dried for when they are out of season or the winter time.

Even today, Crete produces dried grapes (sultanas) of a high quality and dried figs can be found on the market.

## FOODS RICH IN ANTIOXIDATIVE AGENTS

Vegetables and fruit are the main sources of antioxidative agents! They contain vitamins C, E, ß carotene and others which are now believed to play an important role in the prevention of certain types of cancer as well as of atherosclerosis.

Many of these substances which are to be found in vegetables are water soluble and so they dissolve in the water on being cooked.

The Cretan diet has the answer to this: the inhabitants consume a large range of greens and vegetables raw, so gaining the total value!

The consumption of fruit and vegetables on Crete is significantly greater than in those areas which were studied in the "Study of the Seven Countries", as is shown in Table 9.

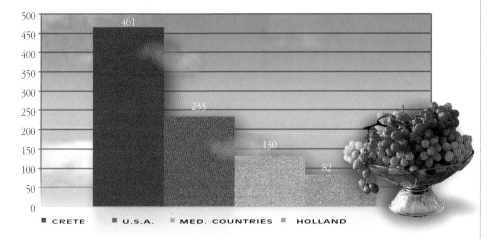

| TABLE 9 | **FRUIT CONSUMPTION** |

- CRETE    - U.S.A.    - MED. COUNTRIES    - HOLLAND

*(Chart values: CRETE 461, U.S.A. 233, MED. COUNTRIES 130, HOLLAND 82)*

# PURSLANE
## *(Portulaca oleracia)*
## A WONDERFUL WEED!

The example of purslane is characteristic of the uniqueness of the Cretan diet. It is a weed which grows in abundance in Mediterranean gardens and spreads at great speed. This is the reason why farmers try to get rid of this weed in many agricultural areas.

There are even special chemicals which dry out and eventually kill this weed. This train of thought is unthinkable to the Cretans! Purslane is one of their favourite summer salad ingredients. Recently it has been found that purslane is extremely rich in fatty substances, like linolenic acid. Sixty per cent of the fats in purslane, according to A. Simopoulou, is linolenic acid. It is now believed that this acid, as well as other fats which are to be found in this plant, provide protection for the heart, act as a shield against coronary diseases and play an important role in the prevention of cancer. "*It is possible that the linolenic acid which is to be found in this plant plays an important role in the good health of the Cretans*", noted Prof. Renaud. According to the Study of the Seven Countries, 2.3% of the calories which Cretans consume are due to the intake of linolenic acid!

Purslane is mainly eaten in its raw state on Crete. In a salad, it is combined with tomatoes, cucumbers, lettuce and parsley or included in a hot salad with eggs and potatoes. A lovely salad with purslane and yoghurt is often seen in rural areas. The plant can even be kept in a jar with olive oil for the winter months.

# HISTORICAL REVIEW

A great many edible plants form part of the Cretan flora, providing a cheap source of food. There has always been a very strong tie between the Cretans of old and Nature, as can be seen in Minoan wall-paintings: a number of plants are represented, some playing an important part in every day life, others in religion. Edible plants were a basic source of food in Minoan times, while other plants were objects of worship. There are still dozens of trees on Crete which are known for their sacred character, a living proof, after all these centuries, of the close relationship that Minoan Cretans had with Nature.

In the years that followed, greens and vegetables were the basic food of the poor and of those who cultivated the land. Some were eaten raw, just as they were picked from the fields, others boiled or cooked in different ways. We don't exactly know how ancient Cretans cooked their greens.

During the years of hardship under the Turkish occupation (1669-1898), the Cretans survived by cultivating the land and by exploiting the natural resources. The farmers fed on greens and vegetables. Foreign visitors who came to the island were shocked to observe this. They could not believe that a whole family could dine only on greens which had been boiled and then olive oil drizzled on top.

## A BREAKFAST OF RICE AND ARTICHOKES!

The ingenuity of the Cretans is even described in accounts written by foreign travellers to the island which have been saved. Robert Pashley ate a wonderful breakfast of rice and artichokes at the Monastery of Gonia.

*A walk in the countryside to gather greens.*

## THE TENDER SHOOTS OF THE VEGETABLES

Sometimes the hospitable Cretans found nothing around them to offer guests to their ill-fated land, apart from some eggs and rusks. Travellers were amazed by the ingenuity of the Cretans who ate almost anything that grew out of the ground, even those plants, which are today considered to be just weeds! For instance, a great impression was made on the Frenchman Olivier (1792), in that the Cretans ate the leaves of green beans, chick peas, courgette flowers, the tender sprouts of many vegetables, the leaves of the mallow plant, the stalks of Smilax aspera, the tender bramble sprouts which were put in salads and capers kept in vinegar as well as many others.

The same person also noted that the Cretans ate okra cooked with olive oil, with spices and with meat. Raulin, who came to Crete during the 19th century, tried okra for the first time in his life in Kritsa. In his book, "Description Physique de l'île de Crete", Paris 1869, he wrote, (page 156):

*"I was a guest of a farmer, Stavrakis Pangalos, at whose house I ate okra for the first time, a fruit of the Hibiscus esculentus, with a fleshy texture and a taste which I did not find to be repugnant. Cretans cook them with meat and eat them in large quantities in autumn."*

The Cretans had found a way to keep some of their garden harvest, so that in winter, they could eat dried or dehydrated courgettes, okra, green beans and many other vegetables. This made life

a great deal easier because as the farming families were self-sufficient, they depended on the production of food items which would be consumed.

Information which we have about the diet and the trade of products during the period when the island was under Turkish occupation is readily available and so allows us to form an accurate picture of the dietary habits of the population. It is without doubt that during this period, the Cretan diet was developed and took the shape of what we know about it today. It is then that tomatoes became a part of meals along with the introduction and great popularity of the red sauces.

Tomatoes gained a steadfast footing in Cretan cuisine within only a few years and became an essential part of Cretan cookery without there having been any prior information about how to use it or any exchange of recipes.

## SALAD GREENS

The greens and vegetables Cretans used to eat were then, as they are today, of excellent quality.

Raw greens were usually used in salads, as an accompaniment to the main dish. Here is a description of the greens used in their raw state in salads:

# Spine chicory
## *(Cichorium spinosum)* "stamnagathi"

The Ancients, so Dioscourides tells us, used it as a remedy. Today it is widely appreciated all over Crete and, once picked, is served with oil and vinegar. It is a thorny bush, but the thorns ("angathia" in Greek) aren't too prickly and the gathering of the small edible green leaves isn't too difficult.

Its name goes back to an old custom on Crete when the water jars were covered with "stamnagathi" ("stamna" means crock), to prevent small insects from getting into the water.

As with all salads on Crete, the preparation depends on the region and the imagination of the housewife: often, this green is mixed with other wild edibles, a little onion (usually spring onion) and dill.

# Wild chicory, dandelion
## *(Cichorium intybus)* "radiki"

A great delicacy: raw, it is always eaten with a shot of vinegar, because of its bitter taste, or boiled, with both oil and vinegar.

# Milk wort
## *(Reichardia picroides)* ("agalatsida")

Known as "galaktitis" in Byzantium, as "galaktida" in the Middle Ages, it is a Cretan herb with a sweetish taste: delicious as a salad with Cretan olive oil, it can also be cooked.

# Vetchling
## (Lathyrus ochrus)
# "papoules"

This plant is also known as "psares" or "kambilies", in Crete. It is a cultivated green, used almost always raw, in salads. Its taste is slightly bitter, and it is most common during Lent.

It is eaten with oil and vinegar, though on the fasting days when oil is forbidden, it is eaten with plain salt. Like raw artichokes, it is also a very common snack ("mezes") enjoyed with "tsikoudia".

# Purslane
## (Portulaca oleracia)
# "glistrida"

In the rest of Greece this plant is more commonly known as "andrakla". A native plant of the island, it is cultivated and appreciated as a summer ingredient for any salad: (see above).

There are many other greens used in their raw state in salads on Crete (for example, the tender shoots of the broad bean plant).

# GREENS PIES
# "Chortopites"

Crete was, and continues to be, famous for its use of greens in pastry. It used to be a winter and springtime preparation, due to the abundance of fresh greens in the countryside.

During summer it was well-nigh impossible to find wild greens to make the pies; so Cretan housewives prepared them with cultivated greens. In the village of Atsipopoulo, in the region of Rethymnon, "chortopites" were made with the tender shoots of wild beets ("vlita"), which grow profusely in all Cretan gardens.

There are a great number of different kinds of pies made with greens. In each part of the island they are prepared with all sorts of different ingredients and in all kinds of shapes.

According to local customs, these pies can be large, medium or small. Cretan pies have always had a unique taste, because their stuffing is made of a rich mixture of wild greens and aromatic herbs.

To achieve the right balance between these two was a delicate operation: Cretan housewives, using their experience and taste, were able to produce pies with a light smell and a distinct taste, where each herb or green was distinct. In some regions, strong aromatic herbs were not used at all.

# Grilled, "ofti" salad

2 medium-sized potatoes
1 onion
1/2 cup olives (preferably "stafidolies" - wrinkled olives)
1 teasp salt
4-5 tbsps olive oil
juice of 1 lemon

Wash the potatoes very well and wrap them in aluminium foil, together with the onion and the olives.

Place them on the embers or under the grill to cook.

When ready, peel the potatoes and the onion, cut them in slices, and, with the olives, serve them in a dish with lemon and oil and salt.

This may be a main course, but may also be served as an accompaniment to other traditional dishes.

# Country salad "Choriatiki"

2 firm tomatoes
2 small cucumbers
1 bell pepper
1 small onion
5-6 olives
100 grams "feta" cheese
(see the chapter on Cheeses)
1 cup roughly chopped purslane
salt
4 tbsps olive oil
1 tbsp vinegar

Rinse the vegetables, chop and place in a salad bowl.

Shake olive oil with salt and vinegar and pour over the salad. Garnish with the olives and the cheese.

(If you want, sprinkle some oregano on the "feta" cheese or place a rusk in chunks on the bottom of the salad bowl).

# Potato and egg salad

3 medium sized
potatoes
5 or 6 eggs
2 tomatoes cut into
slices
1 onion cut into
slices
2 tbsps of finely
chopped parsley
4-5 purslane sprigs
1 small cucumber cut
into slices
1/2 cup olives
1/2 cup olive oil
2 tbsps vinegar
salt, pepper

Wash and boil the potatoes till fork tender, then peel them. Boil the eggs, then peel them, too. Cut both the potatoes and the eggs in slices and put in a salad bowl. Add the tomatoes, the onion, the parsley, the cucumber, the purslane and the olives.

Mix olive oil with vinegar, salt and pepper and drizzle the salad.

# Beetroot salad

1 kilo beetroots
4 or 5 crushed cloves of garlic
300 grams strained yoghurt
1/2 cup roughly ground walnuts
1/2 cup olive oil
salt, 3 tbsps vinegar

Boil the beets, peel them and dice them. Combine the olive oil with the vinegar, the yoghurt, the garlic and the walnuts and pour this over the beets.
Add some salt, mix and let the salad stand in the refrigerator for an hour or so before serving.

# Boiled bulbs of grape hyacinth

1 kilo bulbs ("askordoulaki")
a small bunch of dill
2 or 3 garlic leaves
salt, 1/2 cup olive oil
4-5 tbsps vinegar

Peel the bulbs, like onions, and rinse them in a bowl with water. Boil them twice, 5-6 minutes each time, changing the water. The third time, add salt to the water and when they are cooked, strain them. Finely chop the garlic leaves and the dill, add to the bulbs; then pour the oil and vinegar mixture and stir.
Keep in the refrigerator.

# Purslane salad

300 grams purslane
250 grams strained yoghurt
4 tbsps olive oil
2 or 3 crushed cloves of garlic
the juice of one lemon
salt

Clean, rinse and chop the purslane. Beat the oil with the lemon juice, the garlic, salt and the yoghurt, add the walnuts and pour over the salad. Mix. and keep in the refrigerator before you serve it.

# Leeks in lemon and flour sauce

1 kilo leeks
1/2 cup olive oil
1 cup finely chopped fennel
salt, pepper
1 tbsp flour
the juice of 1-2 lemons

*Leeks, in Greek "prasa", are also called "kendanes" on Crete.*

Clean the leeks, chop them and brown them in the oil. Add fennel, a little salt and pepper and 2 cups water; let this simmer for about three quarters of an hour. Dilute the flour in the lemon juice, add to the pot, stir and cook for a further couple of minutes.

# Leeks
# in tomato sauce

1 kilo leeks
1/2 cup olive oil
1 cup finely chopped celery
salt, pepper
1/2 kilo finely chopped tomatoes

Clean the leeks, chop them and brown them in the oil. Add celery, a little salt and pepper, the tomatoes and 1-2 cups water: let this simmer until cooked, about 45 minutes.

*Both in this recipe and in the preceding one (leeks in lemon and flour sauce), you can add potatoes or snails.*

# Cauliflower
# in egg-lemon sauce

1 medium sized head of
cauliflower
1/2 cup olive oil
1 finely chopped onion
salt, pepper
2 eggs, 2 lemons

Separate the florets, wash them and brown them in the oil with the onion. Cover with water, salt and pepper and cook the cauliflower for about 20 minutes.
Remove from the fire. Beat 2 eggs with the juice of 2 lemons and add a little of the liquid: return to the pot and mix.

*Cauliflower in egg-lemon sauce*

# Cauliflower omelet

1 medium-sized head of cauliflower
4 tbsps olive oil
5-6 eggs
1/2 cup grated cheese (optional)
salt, pepper

Separate the florets, wash them and and boil in salted water. Strain and put in a pan with the oil. Sauté, turning it round until all the water has evaporated.
Beat the eggs with some salt and pepper, and pour over the cauliflower. When the eggs are firm, turn the omelet ("sfuggato") upside down with the help of a large plate and cook on the other side.

# Courgettes
# with eggs

1/2 kilo courgettes
1/2 kilo finely
chopped tomatoes
1/2 cup olive oil
1 onion
salt, pepper
5 eggs

Cut the courgettes in round slices.
Heat olive oil in a shallow saucepan and

brown the onion and the courgettes. Add the tomatoes, salt and pepper; simmer. When the courgettes are cooked, beat the eggs and add them to the saucepan. Stir and let the eggs cook.

## Stuffed courgette flowers (dolmathes)

40 courgette flowers
1/2 kilo rice
1/2 cup olive oil

1/2 kilo ripe tomatoes
1-2 onions
salt, pepper
parsley, mint and fennel
(1 small bunch of each herb)

The flowers have to be picked in the morning so that they will be open. Wash them and prepare the stuffing: chop the parsley, the mint, the fennel leaves, the onions and the tomatoes, very finely. Add the oil, the rice, the salt and pepper and 1/2 cup water: mix. Instead of all the rice, you can use half the quantity and add 300 grams minced meat.

Stuff the flowers and place them in a pot. Cover in water, put a plate over them to keep them from opening and let them simmer until the water has been absorbed.

## Stuffed vine leaves

400 grams vine leaves
1/2 kilo rice
2 or 3 artichoke hearts
2-3 onions
2 or 3 courgettes
2 potatoes
1 cup olive oil
1 lemon
salt, pepper
1 cup finely chopped parsley
1/2 cup finely chopped mint

*Stuffed wine leaves*

Bleach the vine leaves for 5 minutes. Strain them and prepare the stuffing: place the rice in a bowl. Grate the potatoes, the courgettes, the onions, the artichoke hearts: add all this to the rice. Mix with the finely chopped mint, the

parsley, the salt and pepper and the oil. Stuff the vine leaves and place them in a pot. Put a plate over them, cover with water and simmer gently.

Just before removing them from the heat, pour the lemon juice over them.

## Stuffed cabbage leaves (lachanodolmathes)

1 large cabbage
finely chopped parsley, mint,

fennel leaves
(1 small bunch of each)
1/2 kilo rice
4 grated tomatoes
1 cup olive oil
3 grated onions
salt, pepper

Cut out the core of the cabbage, separate the leaves and bleach them for 5 minutes.

Prepare the stuffing with all the ingredients mentioned above. Take each leaf, separate it into 2 parts by severing along the central vein.

Place one spoonful on the bottom centre of each half and roll up towards the top.

Pour 2 tbsps olive oil

*Stuffed cabbage leaves*

in a saucepan, place a layer of shredded cabbage leaves on the bottom and on them, place the "dolmathes" in circles.

Add water to cover them, 2 tbsps of oil and simmer until the water has been absorbed. Now and then, shake the pot to keep the lower cabbage leaves from sticking.

(If desired, some of the rice can be left out and some minced meat added).

# Stuffed vegetables

5 or 6 tomatoes
2 or 3 aubergines
2 or 3 courgettes
2 or 3 bell peppers
2 or 3 potatoes
2 onions
1 cup finely chopped dill or mint
1 cup finely chopped parsley
1 cup of "staka" (fresh goat's butter), optional
1/2 cup olive oil
salt, pepper
1/2 kilo rice
3 grated tomatoes
1 cup grated cheese (optional)

*Stuffed vegetables*

*Cabbage and rice pilaff*

Prepare the **stuffing**: hollow out all the vegetables and chop their contents in a bowl (except for the bell peppers). Add the finely chopped onion, the "staka" butter, 1/4 cup olive oil, the dill, the parsley, the rice, salt and pepper.

Salt the empty insides of the vegetables, stuff them and place them in a deep baking dish. Pour the grated tomatoes and the remaining oil over them. Cook in a hot oven. Just before turning off the oven, sprinkle with the grated cheese and let it melt.

# Cabbage and rice pilaff

1 small cabbage
2 cups rice
1/2 cup olive oil
1/2 kilo tomatoes
1 onion
salt, pepper

Chop the cabbage. Brown the finely chopped onion in the oil. Add the grated tomato, bring to the boil, add the cabbage and the rice and 4 cups of water. Season with salt and pepper.

Simmer until water has been absorbed, stirring occasionally to prevent rice from sticking.

# Spinach and rice pilaff

1 kilo spinach
1 cup finely chopped parsley
1 grated onion
1/2 cup olive oil
1/2 kilo finely chopped tomatoes
1 cup rice
salt, pepper

Wash and chop spinach.

Heat olive oil in a saucepan and sauté onion, spinach and parsley. Add tomato and simmer for 5-6 minutes.

Stir in rice, salt, pepper and 2-3 cups water and simmer until water has been absorbed, stirring occasionally to prevent rice from sticking.

3 grated tomatoes
1 cup rice, 3 cups water
salt, pepper

Trim the ends of the artichokes, rinse them and cut into small cubes. Season with ample salt and leave aside for one hour, then drain on kitchen roll.
Brown the onion in the oil and add the aubergines. Add the tomatoes, let this come to the boil and then pour in the water, salt and pepper.
When the water boils, add the rice and finish cooking until the water has been absorbed, stirring occasionally to prevent the rice from sticking.

# "Koukouvaja" Rusk ("paximathi") with tomato

*A wonderful Cretan appetizer, a common accompaniment to "tsikouthia", the popular alcoholic drink of Crete.*

> 1 rusk
> 1 finely chopped tomato
> 2 tbsps olive oil
> salt, oregano
> 2 tbsps sour myzithra or
> crumbled feta cheese
> (see the chapter on cheeses)

Sprinkle the rusk with very little water to dampen and soften slightly.
Place it on a plate and drizzle with olive oil, tomato, salt, oregano and cheese. Serve immediately.

# Aubergine and rice pilaff

> 1/2 kilo aubergines
> 1/2 cup olive oil
> 1 finely chopped onion

# Artichokes with yoghurt

> 1 kilo artichoke hearts
> 1 finely chopped onion
> 1/2 cup olive oil
> salt, pepper
> 1/2 kilo strained yoghurt

Prepare the artichokes: cut off outer leaves and trim the ends, rub with lemon and cut an incision on the upper side of each.
Heat olive oil in a skillet and brown the onion. Add 1 cup water, the artichokes upside down, salt and pepper. Simmer till the artichokes are tender. Don't stir the artichokes, just shake the pot now and then during the cooking.
Then, add the yoghurt, cook for a further 5 minutes and remove from the heat.

*Artichokes and fresh broad beans*

# Artichokes and fresh broad beans

1 kilo artichokes
1 kilo fresh broad beans
1/2 cup olive oil
2 fresh garlic leaves
1 cup finely chopped dill
or fennel
salt, pepper
2 tbsps flour
2 or 3 tbsps vinegar

Prepare the artichokes: cut off the outer leaves and trim the ends, rub with lemon juice and leave aside. Prepare the broad beans: if they are very tender, keep both the broad beans and the pods cutting off the edges and the fibres from both sides. If they are too big, discard the pods.

Heat olive oil in a saucepan and sauté garlic and dill or fennel for 5 minutes. Add broad beans and 2 cups water and simmer for a quarter of an hour. Add artichokes, salt, pepper and cover with water. Simmer and when the food is almost cooked, take some of the liquid which you gently add to the flour diluted in some water. Add the vinegar and pour this thick batter back into the pot, shaking the pot to mix the batter properly with the food. Cook for another 5-6 minutes and the dish is ready.

# Artichoke omelet

5-6 artichoke hearts
3-4 tbsps olive oil
5 eggs
1/2 cup grated cheese
salt, pepper

Cut off the outer leaves of the artichokes, trim the ends, boil in salted water for 10 minutes and strain.
Heat olive oil in a frying pan, add chopped artichokes and sauté until their water has

evaporated, stirring occasionally with a wooden spoon.

Beat the eggs, add salt, pepper and the cheese and pour the mixture over the artichokes. When the eggs are firm, turn the "sfuggato" around with the help of a large plate and cook on the other side until golden brown.

# Courgettes with garlic in tomato sauce

1,5 kilos small courgettes
7 or 8 cloves of garlic, finely chopped
1/2 cup finely chopped parsley
1/2 cup olive oil
1/2 kilo tomatoes
salt, pepper

Wash the courgettes and slit them with a knife. Put garlic in the slits and place the courgettes in a baking dish. Add the oil and the grated tomato, sprinkle with parsley, salt and pepper and bake for an hour or so in a moderate oven.

# "Sofegatha"

This is a wholesome Cretan dish which seems to have its origin in Venetian times. The word "sofegada" occurs in some texts of the time and experts believe it was originally some kind of meat dish. What we do know is that it was evidently cooked in its own steam, "suffocated", if we are to believe its Venetian etymology. The word has survived in Eastern Crete, though not to describe a meat dish. On the contrary, this is a dish based on garden produce, as we shall see further on. In Western Crete the name is unknown: some elderly people vaguely remember it, but have forgotten its meaning.

Until recently, it was prepared with the last produce from the garden at the end of summer. In the autumn, there were less quantities of vegetables and the gardener who found his daily nourishment in the produce of his garden, had to do with whatever there was: 2 courgettes, 1 aubergine...

Having no choice but to cook this, and on discovering that the result was satisfactory, "sofegada" became a very pleasant summer dish, also prepared when there is an abundance of vegetables.

### Ingredients:

200 grams aubergines
200 grams courgettes
200 grams fresh beans
2-3 green peppers
4-5 green beet leaves
5-6 courgette flowers
2 potatoes
1 kilo tomatoes
2 onions
1 cup olive oil
salt, pepper

Rinse vegetables.
Brown the chopped onion in the oil. Add the courgettes, the beans, the aubergines ,cut into chunks.
Sauté for 5 minutes and add the sliced green peppers, the finely chopped tomatoes, the sliced potatoes and finally the courgette flowers with the chopped green beet leaves. Add salt, pepper, 2 cups water and simmer for about one hour until water has been absorbed.

# Courgette balls

1 kilo courgettes
1/2 kilo potatoes
1 kilo onions
2 or 3 eggs
1 cup grated cheese
1 teaspoon salt
flour and olive oil for frying

Boil, and then strain, the courgettes, the potatoes and the onions. (Squeeze them through a cotton cloth for better results). Combine with the eggs, the cheese and salt. Shape the balls, dredge with flour and deep-fry on both sides until golden brown. Place on kitchen roll so that oil will be absorbed and serve.

*Courgette pie*

# Courgette pie from Chania

1 kilo courgettes cut in fine round slices
1 kilo potatoes cut in fine round slices
salt, pepper
1/2 cup finely chopped mint
1 kilo "galomyzithra"
(see the chapter on cheeses)
1/2 cup olive oil

For the **dough:**
1/2 kilo flour
3 tbsps olive oil
the juice of 1 lemon
1 cup water
1 teasp salt

With the above ingredients prepare the dough and roll out 2 "phyllo" sheets.
Oil a baking pan, spread out one sheet and on it, place all the salted ingredients in layers.
That is first potatoes, then "myzithra" and mint, the third layer with courgettes and the fourth with "myzithra" and mint again. Finally place the second "phyllo" sheet over the last layer, sprinkle with 1/2 cup olive oil and sesame seeds, score the portions with a knife and bake in the oven.

# Large spinach-and-greens pie

1,5 kilos greens
(wild greens, spinach, fennel, parsley, dill, mint, leeks etc.)
1/2 cup olive oil
2 finely chopped onions
salt, pepper

For the **dough**:
1/2 kilo flour
1/2 cup water
1/2 cup olive oil
2 tbsps lemon juice
1 teaspoon salt
(*Commercial "phyllo"
can also be used*)
1 egg
sesame seeds

# Fried small spinach-and-greens pies

1 kilo wild greens and spinach
1 cup finely chopped parsley
1/2 cup finely chopped mint
1 dried finely chopped onion or
2-3 spring onions
1/2 cup olive oil
salt, pepper
For the **dough:** 1/2 kilo flour
1 cup water
2-3 tbsps olive oil
1 teaspoon salt
2-3 tbsps lemon juice
olive oil for frying

Sauté onion and greens in the oil and strain for 3-4 hours. Salt and pepper. Prepare the dough with the above ingredients and divide into 3-4 parts. Roll each one out, 1/2 cm thick. Cut out 10 cm circles and place 1 tbsp of the mixture on each circle. Fold and close the edges firmly, pressing them down with a fork.

Deep fry in olive oil until golden brown on both sides. Place on kitchen roll so that the oil can be absorbed.

Rinse and chop greens.

Heat olive oil in a pot and sauté onions and greens for 20 minutes. Add salt and pepper.

Make a dough with the warm water, the oil, the salt, the lemon juice and the flour and roll out 2 "phyllo" sheets, the size of the baking pan.

Spread one sheet on the bottom of the oiled baking pan: on this, spread the greens. Cover with the second sheet, dab with beaten egg, sprinkle with sesame seeds and bake until golden brown.

*("Feta" cheese may be added to the mixture of greens)*

# Baked small spinach-and-greens pies

Prepare the stuffing and the dough exactly as in the above recipe.

Divide the dough into 3-4 balls and roll each one out, 1/2 cm thick. Cut out 10-12 cm circles and place 1 tbsp of the mixture on each circle. Fold and close the edges firmly, dab with beaten egg, sprinkle with sesame seeds and bake in the oven until golden brown, about half an hour.

# Courgette souflé

1,5 kilos courgettes
3 cups milk
1/2 cup olive oil
1/2 kilo "feta" cheese or any other cheese
3 eggs
1 cup semolina
salt
1/2 teaspoon grated nutmeg

Grate the courgettes, salt them and let

them stand for 5-6 hours.

Beat the olive oil wth the eggs, the milk, the cheese and the semolina until you get a thick mash.

When the courgettes have got rid of most of their liquid, mix them with the mash and place the mixture in an oiled baking pan. Bake in the oven for about an hour, until golden brown.

# Spinach pie

**Stuffing:**
1,5 kilos spinach
1/2 cup olive oil
1 finely chopped onion
1/2 kilo feta cheese
4 eggs
salt, pepper

For the **dough**:
1/2 cup olive oil
the juice of one lemon
1 teaspoon dry active yeast
1 teaspoon salt
1 cup water
about 700 grams flour

Prepare the dough: dilute the yeast in warm water, add the oil, the salt, the lemon juice and the flour. Knead the dough and let it stand for a couple of hours.

In the meantime, prepare the stuffing: wash and chop the spinach and sauté it in the oil with the onion for 10-15 minutes. Strain it and add the feta cheese, some salt, pepper and the beaten eggs.

Roll out 2 sheets of dough and spread one sheet on the bottom of an oiled baking pan.

Place the stuffing on it and cover with the other sheet. Brush the top with olive oil and bake in the oven until golden brown, in about one hour.

*Small fried pumpkin pies*

# Spinach rolls

For the **stuffing**:
1 kilo spinach
1/2 cup olive oil
1/2 kilo "xinomyzithra"
(see the chapter on cheeses)
3 eggs
salt, pepper, grated nutmeg
1/2 kilo of commercial paper-thin
pastry

Wash and chop the spinach, salt it and let it stand overnight. Next morning, drain it and brown it in the oil until the water evaporates.

Add the mashed "myzithra" and the beaten eggs, a little grated nutmeg and some pepper. Oil 4 or 5 sheets of pastry; place some of the stuffing along one edge and roll up. In the same manner, roll up the rest of the pastry with the stuffing and place each roll, one next to the other, in the baking pan. Brush with fresh butter or olive oil and bake till golden brown.

# Small fried pumpkin pies

**Stuffing:**
2 or 3 kilos pumpkin
1/2 cup olive oil
2 finely chopped onions
salt, pepper, cumin

The **dough**:
1 kilo flour
1,5 cups water
2 teaspoons salt
5-6 tbsps olive oil
1 tbsp vinegar
olive oil for frying

Cut the pumpkin into cubes and sauté with the finely chopped onion in the oil. Stir the pumpkin from time to time as it is cooking until all the water has evaporated and it has become mushy. Drain it and add salt, pepper and quite a lot of cumin.
Prepare

# Small onion pies

**For the filling:**
1 kilo onions cut in fine slices
3 finely chopped tomatoes
100 grams crumbled
"feta" cheese
1/2 cup olive oil
salt, pepper
**For the dough:**
1/2 kilo flour
1 cup water
4 tbsps olive oil
the grated peel and
juice of 1 lemon
1/2 teaspoon salt

Brown the onions in the oil and add the tomatoes, salt and pepper. Simmer until the sauce thickens and add the cheese. Prepare the dough with the above ingredients and roll it out 1/2 cm thick. Cut out 10 cm circles and place 1 teaspoon mixture on each circle. Fold forming semi-circular pies and close the edges firmly, pressing them down with a fork. Deep fry in olive oil until golden brown on both sides. Place on kitchen roll so that the oil can be absorbed.

*Pumpkin pie*

the dough with the above ingredients and roll it out 1/2 cm thick.

Cut out 10 cm circles and place 1 tbsp of the mixture on each circle. Fold and close the edges firmly, pressing them down with a fork.

Deep fry in olive oil until golden brown on both sides. Place on kitchen roll so that the oil is absorbed.

Cut the pumpkin into cubes and sauté it with the onion in the oil till mushy.

Drain well, then add mint, crumbled "feta" cheese and the beaten eggs.

Prepare the dough and roll out 2 sheets. Spread one sheet on an oiled baking pan, spread the mixture on it, and on top, the second sheet.

Brush with olive oil or beaten egg and bake till golden brown.

# Pumpkin pie

1,5 kilos pumpkin
2 finely chopped onions
salt, pepper
1/2 cup finely chopped mint
1/2 kilo "feta" cheese
2 or 3 eggs

The **dough**: 1 cup olive oil
2 eggs
1 teaspoon salt
1/2 cup milk
1 teaspoon baking
powder
as much flour as needed
(more or less 1 kilo)

# THE HERBS OF CRETE

Aromatic plants and herbs play an important role in Cretan life. The land is one of the richest places in the world for indigenous plants! These plants were often used in the Cretan cuisine. Sometimes they were used to flavour different products, such as edible olives and olive oil, other times they were used to make a dish much more tasty and at other times, they were used to make teas which were frequently drunk. Botanical studies have shown that the island has one of the most interesting eco-systems in Europe and that many of the indigenous plants have been used not only in traditional folklore medicine, but also in pharmaceuticals!

In the villages, anyone can find a great number of herbs, some with a strong and distinct while others with a less potent smell and taste. There are still many people, usually of the older generation, who can recognise a lot of herbs, know which season they should collect them and always have a magnificently well-stocked house of herbs! Some of these have grown accustomed to selling small bags with herbs and aromatic plants. In the last few years, several companies have been set up which collect, process and package, in lovely combinations, some of the Cretan herbs. Among those plants is the famous Dittany (Origanum dictamnus), a plant which grows only on Crete, oregano (Origanum onites), marjoram (Origanum majorana), thyme (Thymus capitatus) and sage (Salvia fruticosa). Herbs are a valuable ally in achieving and maintaining good health as they contain large amounts of antioxidative agents.

## Dittany (Origanum dictamnus)

This plant re-sows itself in the mountains of Crete, mainly in remote spots where it grows in larger quantities as it is not easy for plant eating animals to reach it!

In ancient times, doctors believed that it cured all illnesses! It was especially useful for women who were convinced that it helped in the process of giving birth. Many ancient writers mention that it worked wonders on wounds. It was believed that if a wild goat was hit by a hunter and the arrow stayed in its body, then it would run off to find dittany to eat so as to heal the wound! Even the goddess of love, Aphrodite, is said to have come to the island of Crete in order to get some dittany to use as a medicine. On Crete, it was always seen as a plant of love. They believed that the plant itself encouraged feelings of love.

In ancient times it was the most usual present to be exchanged between lovers!

## Oregano (Origanum onites)

This well known aromatic plant is used in folklore medicine, in the form of a tea, as a cure for diarrhoea. But it is mostly used in different kinds of food (roasted potatoes in olive oil and oregano) or a little is sprinkled on the much loved "daco" (a dry rusk with olive oil and finely chopped tomatoes), which is one of the most popular Cretan appetizers.

## "Sage"
## (Salvia fruticosa)

This is a well known herb with a strong smell and taste. It grows nearly all over the island and is ingeniously used in folklore medicine for cases of colds or stomach problems. It is generally considered to be a tonic and is drunk in the form of a tea with honey. The ethereal oil from this plant is especially good at reducing toothache.

## Rosemary
## (Rosmarinus officinalis)

This is a well loved herb and many Cretans still cultivate bushes of this aromatic plant in pots. In the old days, it was a useful ally of good health as it was frequently put to use as a folklore medicinal remedy, such as an antiseptic, a relief for headaches, eyes, the stomach and the back, as well as being a herb which stopped hair loss and instead, produced lovely, shiny hair! It was also used as an effective beauty product in the upkeep not only of hair, but also of the face and the skin.

On Crete it is greatly used in cooking. This is the herb which gives a characteristic smell and taste to "savore", marinated dishes. Fish, snails or "liver savore", are well known all over the island!

# HERB TEAS

## DITTANY TEA

It is the most common tea drunk by the Cretans. A small amount of Dittany leaves are boiled in water for 2-3 minutes. The liquid is then strained of the leaves and the tea is ready. Like everyday tea, it is available in tea bags. These bags can be placed in boiled water but they need at least 5 minutes to fuse so that the drink is aromatic. Although this tea does not have a strong colour, it more than makes up for it with its taste!

## SAGE TEA

Sage is boiled in water as is done with most herbs. As it has a strong taste and goes bitter, only a small amount is required.

## A MIXTURE OF HERBS

The mixture of herbs which is used for tea includes 8 different herbs and is known in many areas of Crete as "karteraki".
This tea has no definite taste as it depends on the choice of herbs and the amount of each one in the total mixture. We could say that the taste is a case of personal preference and local availability (some areas use more camomile whereas others use more dittany).

▶ **WARNING**: *the mixing of herbs with very a strong smell (like sage) with others, should be avoided, as the strong smell covers the smell of the others. This is the reason why sage should be used in very small amounts in herb mixtures.*

## Braised chicken with sage

*Chicken can be cooked with sage. The combination is rather successful, as it makes the chicken tastier and gives it an unusual herbal flavour.*

*Recipe continued on p. 125*

# Braised chicken with sage

1 medium-sized chicken
1 finely chopped onion
1/2 cup olive oil
1/2 cup white wine
the juice of 1 lemon
salt, 2 sage sprigs

Wash the chicken and cut into serving pieces, removing skin and fat, if you want. Heat olive oil in a saucepan and sauté the onion and the chicken, turning it on all sides to brown evenly. Pour in wine and 1 cup water and simmer until tender. Add lemon juice, salt and sage 5 minutes before removing the pan from the fire.

Rinse liver and cut into pieces. Season with salt and pepper. Heat olive oil in a frying pan, dredge liver pieces with flour and fry on all sides. Place on kitchen roll so that the oil is absorbed.

Strain the frying oil, put it back into the pan and heat. Add vinegar and rosemary and pour over the fried liver.

# Braised chicken with oregano

1 medium chicken
1 finely chopped onion
1/2 cup olive oil
the juice of 1-2 lemons
salt, 1 tbsp oregano

Rinse the chicken and cut into serving portions. Leave the chicken pieces in salted water for 4 hours and take off the skin.

Heat olive oil in a saucepan and sauté the onion and the chicken, turning it on all sides to brown evenly. Pour in lemon juice, oregano, a little salt and 2 cups water. Simmer until the chicken is tender and most water has evaporated.

# Marinated liver ("savore") with rosemary

1 kilo liver
salt, pepper
1 cup flour
1 cup olive oil
4 tbsps vinegar
1 tbsp rosemary

# Baked pilchard with oregano

1 kilo pilchards
5-6 tbsps olive oil
the juice of 2 lemons
2 teaspoons oregano
salt, pepper

Gut and rinse pilchard. Place in an oiled baking dish and season with salt, pepper and oregano. Douse with olive oil and lemon juice and bake first at high temperature for 20 minutes and then at medium temperature for 30 minutes more.

# Marinated red mullet

1 kilo red mullets
1/2 cup olive oil
flour and olive oil for frying
100 ml white wine
2 tbsps vinegar
2 tbsps rosemary

*Right: Baked pilchard with oregano*

*Marinated red mullet*

Scale, gut and rinse the fish. Add salt and leave aside for 1 hour.

Heat olive oil in a frying pan, dredge fish with flour and fry until golden brown on both sides. Place on kitchen roll so that the oil is absorbed.

Strain the frying oil, put it back into the pan and heat. Add 1 tbsp flour, wine, vinegar, salt, pepper and rosemary. Stir for a couple of minutes and pour the sauce over the fried mullets.

*Fish prepared in this way can be preserved for a few days.*

# Dried beans with fennel leaves

1/2 kilo dried beans
(preferably "mavromatika")
1/2 cup olive oil
300 grams finely chopped fennel
1 finely chopped onion
1 tbsp concentrated tomato pulp
or 1/2 kilo finely chopped
tomatoes
salt, pepper

Boil the beans for quarter of an hour and then drain them.

Heat olive oil in a pot and sauté the onion and the fennel. Stir in the tomatoes and simmer for 10 minutes. Add the beans, salt, pepper and water to cover them and simmer till water is absorbed and the sauce thickens.

# Cuttlefish with fennel

1 kilo cuttlefish
1/2 cup olive oil
1 dried onion or 2-3 spring onions, finely chopped
1/2 cup dry white wine
1/2 kilo finely chopped fennel
1/2 kilo grated tomatoes
salt, pepper

Clean the cuttlefish: remove the eyes, the single bone, the stomach and the ink. Rinse well and cut into strips.

Brown the onion in the oil and add the cuttlefish.

Cook for 15 minutes, stirring occasionally, until all liquid has been absorbed. Pour in the wine, fennel, tomatoes, salt, pepper and 2 cups water. Simmer until most liquid has been absorbed and fennel and cuttlefish are cooked.

# Cheese pies "kallitsounia" with mint from Chania

The **dough**: 1 kilo flour
1/2 cup olive oil
the juice of 1 lemon
1/2 teaspoon crushed coriander
1/2 teaspoon crushed mastic
1 teaspoon salt
2 cups water or "alousia"
(*water in which some ashes, tied in a clean cloth, have been boiled*)
The **stuffing**: 2 kilos "malaka" and "galomyzithra" (*see chapter on cheeses*), 1 or 2 eggs
2 tbsps finely chopped mint

Prepare the dough with the above ingredients and leave aside for one hour. Mix myzithra with eggs and mint.

Roll out the dough, 1/2 cm thick and proceed to cut out 10 cm circles. Place 1 tbsp myzithra on each circle, fold and close the edges firmly. Dab with beaten egg, sprinkle with sesame seeds and bake in the oven until golden brown, for about half an hour.

# PULSES

**P**ulses have been known about and included in the every day diet since antiquity. Minoans used to make offerings of pulses and cereals to their gods, to show their gratitude for the fertility of the earth, as the seeds planted and nourished by the earth were returned manifold. Some telling customs have remained with us to this day: the habit Cretan peasants have of cooking together all the kinds of pulses once a year goes way back to Antiquity. Every member of the family partakes of this mixture of pulses, then the animals of the house and finally a handful is flung onto the roof of the house, for the birds.

Civilisation took a great step forward with the systematic cultivation of cereals and pulses: these could be stored, providing nourishment on the days when, for one reason or another (weather, illness), it proved impossible to go out in search of food.

In more recent times, the ways of preparing pulses were greatly varied: each dish related to the local produce and so very often, pulses were cooked with meat. These local customs, among other things, have a definite folkloric value.

## PULSES WITH VEGETABLES
## AND OTHER FANTASTIC COMBINATIONS

**P**ulses are a pillar of the Cretan diet. They are eaten in large amounts, especially during the winter months. Their easy storage and relatively simple cultivation needs, made them a popular food source in ancient civilisations. Carbonised pulses have been found in archaeological digs on Crete and even in settlements from 2000 B.C.. In the traditional cuisine, pulses are cooked in various ways, with either meat or salted cod, or with rice to make such dishes as rice and lentils or beans and rice.

In addition, traditional weddings have a particular dish which uses pulses and this is served for dinner on the eve or the

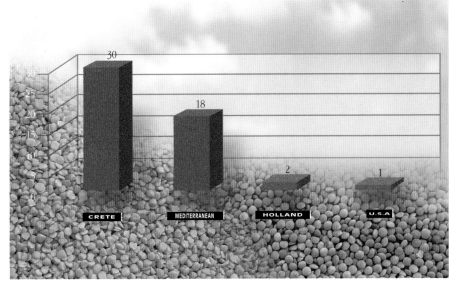

**CONSUMPTION OF PULSES (grams per day)**

day before the eve of the wedding. It was usually meat with chick peas. The most interesting way of cooking pulses on the island of Crete is when they are combined with local greens and vegetables. These produce impressively wonderful flavours and a high standard of gastronomy as well as giving some great ideas on a balanced diet! Chick peas with spinach, beans with fennel, broad beans with wild artichokes along with the well known fava which is served with caper. Pulses are often flavoured with parsley, french onions, celery and are accompanied with carrot and a range of local greens. It seems that the Cretans have yet another part of the jigsaw in the protective shield of good health.

These greens can provide a great amount of antioxidative agents.

The study of the seven countries showed that the Cretans consume 30 grams of pulses every day on average in comparison to 18 grams which are consumed by the inhabitants of the other Mediterranean areas. In the northern countries, the amount of pulses consumed comes to just 2 grams per day, while in USA, there is hardly any intake of pulses, at a mere 1 gram per day. (Table 10 )

# SOAKED BROAD BEANS
## (*Vrechtokoukia*)

*An indispensable dish during the periods of fasting imposed by the Orthodox Church, especially on the days when it is forbidden to consume oil.*

*Until recently, these beans were always served on "Kathari Deftera" (the Monday after Carnival, the first day of Lent). They, too, are one of the most common snacks ("mezes") that accompany a glass of "tsikoudia" (Crete's traditional form of spirits).*

*Lupins, "thermoi" in ancient Greek. A common food product during fasting periods.*

No particular preparation is required for "vrechtokoukia": just soak the beans overnight, in salted water, in an earthenware or metal container.

Next morning they're ready to be eaten, usually with some olives (of the kind called in Crete "alatsolies" or "stafidoelies") and some rusks ("paximadi").

# Lupins

T hese beans were famous in Antiquity and were called "thermos". They have been in use in the Greek world since then. They were the usual fare of the cynical philosophers in ancient Greece, they also were the main dish of the "dinners of Hecate": on the last day of every month, once the houses had been thoroughly cleaned, the table was set and Hecate's dinner served so as to placate the goddess of ghosts.

In front of each house the dinner was placed on a tripod (the goddess was always represented on a tripod): any

passer-by was welcome to this dinner, so naturally all the poor people waited impatiently for this occasion. Ever since, these beans have been identified as a poor man's fare.

Ancient Greeks prepared lupins, or "thermos", in exactly the same way as they do on Crete nowadays: first, they are boiled, then they are left in salted water for 2 or

*Collecting the leguminous plants for pulses*

3 days to get rid of their bitterness. They're served during the periods of fasting, with olives and Cretan rusks.

# «Palikaria»
## (a mixture of many pulses)

They're also known as "psarokolyva" and "mayeria". This mixture of pulses is a very old custom, reminiscent of the "panspermia" known in Ancient Greece, reminiscent, too, of the Minoan offerings to the gods. For all we know, it might go back to pre-historical times, for which there are no written sources. In ancient Greece "panspermia" was an offering to the gods: to Apollo on the 7th day of the "Pyanepsion", to "Chthonios" Hermes (Mercury of the Underworld) and to the dead during the "Anthestiria"; it was also prepared on the day of "Chytri" and during the feast of "Thargilia". A few of all the new seeds were boiled together and offered to the gods in gratitude for the plentiful new crops. This dish was served at the table of every ancient Greek family and every member partook of it.

On Crete, this custom survived through the centuries. In the eastern part of the island, this dish was known as "palikaria", a word which may well derive from the ancient name "polisporia" (which means: many seeds). It was cooked on the 5th of January, the day before the feast of the Baptism of Christ. All the family and the animals of the house shared this meal, in particular the animals used for farming. On this day, the old women in the region of Pediada, still fling a plateful of this mixture on to the

*roof of the houses, for the birds. On this occasion men and animals share the same meal....*

*In some Cretan villages, "palikaria" or "polisporia" is prepared on the eve of the feast of the Epiphany (the Baptism of Christ and the Blessing of the Waters) and during Lent. The only difference is that the pulses are served with oil, finely chopped parsley or dill and fresh onion.*

To **prepare** this dish:

100 grams chick peas
100 grams wheat
100 grams dried beans
100 grams millet
100 grams lentils
100 grams peas

To serve:
dried or spring onion
finely chopped dill
olive oil
lemon juice
salt
pepper

Soak all pulses in water overnight; place wheat and chick peas in a separate bowl, as they need more time in cooking. Lentils or split peas do not need to be soaked at all.

The next day put enough water in a large pot and boil wheat and chickpeas first for half an hour.

Add remaining pulses and continue boiling until the pulses are soft. Add salt and pepper and serve either as a soup in its own juices or strained as a salad with olive oil, a sprinkling of finely chopped dill and finely chopped onion, to desired taste.

# Dried beans with spinach

1/2 kilo dried beans
1 kilo spinach
1 finely chopped onion
1/2 cup olive oil
1 cup finely chopped dill or fennel
1/2 kilo finely chopped tomatoes
salt
pepper

Rinse and chop spinach.

Put the beans in a large pot with ample salted water and boil for half an hour; then strain.

In the same pot sauté the onion and the fennel in the oil for 10 minutes.

Add the beans, the tomatoes, salt, pepper and 2-3 cups water and simmer until almost cooked. Add spinach 15 minutes before removing the pot from the heat.

*Dried beans with spinach*

## Dried beans in tomato sauce

1/2 kilo dried beans
1 finely chopped onion
1/2 cup olive oil
1/2 kilo finely chopped tomatoes
1/2 cup finely chopped celery
1/2 cup finely chopped parsley
2-3 medium carrots in round slices or diced
salt, pepper

Put the beans in a large pot with ample salted water and boil for half an hour; then strain.

In the same pot heat the oil and brown the onion until translucent.

Add the celery, the parsley, the carrots, the tomatoes, salt, pepper and 2-3 cups water.

When all this comes to the boil, add the beans and simmer until the sauce thickens.

## Dried beans in lemon-flour sauce

1/2 kilo dried beans
1-2 finely chopped onions
1/2 cup olive oil
salt, pepper
1 tbsp flour
juice of
1 lemon

Put the beans in a large pot with ample salted water and boil for half an hour; then strain.

In the same pot sauté the onion in the oil until translucent.

Add the beans, salt, pepper and water to cover and simmer until cooked.

Dissolve the flour in the lemon juice and add it to the pot. Simmer for a further 5-6 minutes stirring occasionally and the food is ready.

The consistency should be that of a soup.

# VIRGIN MARY'S BEAN AND RICE PILAFF

This dish was prepared until a few years ago in the village of Piscopiano, northern Crete on 21st November, the day of the Presentation of Virgin Mary.

It has its origin in ancient "polycarpia" the ritual dish prepared in ancient Greece in the Autumn, after the harvest, as an expression of thanks to the gods.

## Dried bean and rice pilaff

This was not, generally speaking, a main course dish on Crete. It was simply a way of using up the left-over beans. For the sake of variety, rice was added, giving the dish another taste.

After having half cooked 1 cup of rice in water, the beans were added and the rice cooked through.

Since this is a savoury and wholesome dish, you don't need to have left-over beans to prepare it.

First cook the beans. Remove them from the pot and in their own liquid, cook the rice, adding a little water.

Finally, add the beans with the rice and stir.

## Chick pea and rice pilaff

> 300 grams chick peas
> 1 finely chopped onion
> 1/2 cup olive oil
> 1/2 kilo finely chopped tomatoes
> 1 cup rice
> salt, pepper

Soak chickpeas in water overnight. The next day strain them.

In a large pot, heat olive oil and brown onion until translucent. Add chickpeas, tomatoes and enough water to cover. Simmer until almost cooked (one hour or so). Make sure that there are at

*Chick pea and rice pilaff*

# Broad bean purée

1/2 kilo dried broad
beans
olive oil,
according to taste
salt
the juice of 1 lemon

Soak the beans in water
overnight.
The next day remove the
black tips (the eyes) and
most husks from the beans.
Then boil them in ample
salted water for half an
hour.
Strain and put them again in
the pot with enough water
to cover them. Boil for another half hour.
Towards the end, when the
water is almost gone, you
need to stir the beans often.
Add lemon juice and
remove the pot from the
heat.
Serve with oil and, if desired, with finely chopped
dill and spring onion.

a small bunch finely
chopped parsley (optional)
1 teaspoon cumin
3 or 4 bay leaves
salt, pepper

Soak the beans in water overnight. The
next day remove the black tips (the eyes)
with a sharp knife, boil in ample water
for half an hour and strain.
Brown the onion in the oil and add the
tomatoes, the parsley, the cumin, the bay
leaves, salt and pepper.
Cook for 5 minutes and then add the
boiled beans and 2-3 cups water. Simmer
till the sauce thickens.

# Split pea purée (fava)

2 cups split peas
5 cups water
1 onion quartered
1 teaspoon salt
olive oil, to desired taste

Put split peas in salted water and simmer.
The lid must not sit tightly because the
yellow lentil expands and can spill.
When most water has gone, stir often
until it becomes mushy.
Serve the purée with oil, raw onion and
olives.

least 3 cups of liquid in the pot and add
rice, salt and pepper.
Allow it to cook for another 15 minutes,
stirring from time to time, to prevent it
from sticking.

# Broad bean stew

1/2 kilo dried beans
2 finely chopped onions
2 finely chopped tomatoes
1/2 cup olive oil

# "Married" split pea purée

the left-over split pea purée
(1 cup)
1 onion
5 tbsps olive oil
2 tomatoes
salt, pepper, cumin

*When there was some "fava" left, it
was neither discarded nor was it*

*served again: a completely new dish was prepared on its basis. This is one example of the creativity typical of the Cretan housewives, always finding wonderful means for producing new dishes with new tastes. The expression "to marry the "fava" was common in the region of Sitia.*

Finely chop the onion, brown it in the oil, add the chopped tomatoes, salt, pepper and cumin.
Cook for 10-15 minutes, then add the "fava". Cook a little longer, serve.

# Chick peas in lemon-flour sauce

1/2 kilo chick peas
1/2 cup olive oil
1 finely chopped onion
2 lemons
1 tbsp flour
salt
pepper

Soak the chick peas overnight in water.

The next day, rinse them and add them to a pot in which you have browned the onion in the oil. Add water to cover them, salt, pepper and simmer till cooked, about 1 hour.
Mix the lemon juice with the flour and ten minutes before the peas are cooked, add the mixture to the pot and stir.

# Chick peas in tomato sauce

1/2 kilo chick peas
1/2 cup olive oil
1 finely chopped onion
1/2 kilo finely chopped tomatoes
salt, pepper

Soak the peas overnight and on the following day rinse and strain them.
Heat olive oil in a pot and brown the onion.
Add the chickpeas, the tomato, salt, pepper and water to cover them. Simmer till chickpeas are cooked and the sauce thickens, 1 hour more or less.

# Lentil soup

1/2 kilo lentils
1/2 cup olive oil
1/2 kilo grated tomatoes
1 finely chopped onion
2 or 3 cloves of garlic
3 bay leaves
3 tbsps vinegar
salt, pepper

*Lentil soup*

Fill a pot with plenty of water. Add the lentils and boil them for 10 minutes, then strain.

Brown the finely chopped onion in the oil, add the lentils, the garlic, the tomatoes, water to cover them, salt, pepper and the bay leaves.

Allow the lentils to cook for half an hour.

Pour in vinegar 5 minutes before removing the pot from the fire.

# "Fava" croquettes

1/2 kilo "fava"
1 onion
a small bunch of parsley
1 cup of bread (or rusk) crumbs
1 cup grated cheese
2 eggs
salt, pepper
flour and olive oil for frying

Prepare the "fava" as in the above recipe (split pea purée).

Let it cool, then add the grated onion, the finely chopped parsley, the crumbs, the cheese, the beaten eggs, salt, pepper. Mix well and shape the balls, more long than round. Dredge them with flour and deep-fry until golden brown on both sides. Place on kitchen roll so that the oil can be absorbed and then serve.

# CRETAN TRADITIONAL BREAD

**I**t is a saying on Crete that: "food is the yarn in the stomach and bread is the shuttle". And indeed bread has always been extremely important to Cretans. Sometimes the word "bread" implies the whole meal: "-Come and eat bread with us" is an invitation to lunch. No meal can be conceived without it. There has always been a great variety of breads, according to the season and according to the different feasts, adding to the general enjoyment of the meals. This love of bread is nothing new: first-rate cereals were cultivated in the plains of the island and on the terraces of the mountainous regions way back in antiquity and Minoans stored large amounts of cereals in the warehouses of their palaces.

Bread played a very specific role in every day life in ancient Greece: the flour was kneaded with water, or with water and honey, sometimes with oil or with a special drink made with honey and vinegar or wine. The variety of breads in ancient Greece was really impressive: it had to do with the kind of flour used (barley or wheat), the dough, the manner of preparing it and the shape. The main types of cooking bread were the following:

-bread baked in the oven (**"klivanitis"** from "klivanos" which means oven)
-a thin bread cooked on the grate **("escharitis"** from "schara", the grate)
-bread cooked in a special pot, floating on water (**"plytos"** from "pleo", to float)
-bread cooked on coals ("**apopyrias**" from "pyr", fire)
-bread basted in oil ("**alifalitis**" from "alifo", to baste)

The variety in shape was even greater: oblong, round, semi-circular, flat.
During the Middle Ages, on Crete, there was again a great variety of bread, according to the dough (with water, honey or milk), and the manner of baking. "Bread", too, was a generic word, meaning simply food.
In more recent years the varieties of bread have evolved from the every day life of the inhabitants of the island. Bread was made of barley, wheat or both and sometimes baked into rusks. There were also the celebration breads as well as other specific kinds of bread which are of particular interest.
The custom of preparing holy breads for rituals goes back to
Minoan times. On one of the sarcophagi found in Aghia Triatha in the region of Messara one can see how important bread was in everyday life as well as in the worship of those times, according to specific researchers (according to others, the offered products

*In front of a lit oven in the village of Petrokefali in Messara*

are fruit): a basket of bread is represented next to a bird and beside the famous sacred tree of the Minoans. These are the gifts offered to the gods: the fruits of the new crop. Exactly the same custom is still to be seen nowadays all over the Greek world: the faithful regularly take a special kind of bread to church to be blessed. In both cases, then and now, the bread is a bloodless offering to the divinity. The most common of these holy breads were called "popana", small round breads kneaded in a special fashion. Aristophanes mentions them:

*"After this, he walked round the altars, on which lay the "popana"*
*(Plato, 678-680).*

Several genuine ancient Greek customs related to celebration breads survived on Crete right up to the middle of our century. Minoans, as we said before, offered the first breads of the new year to the gods. The Greeks of the classic period offered their gods a bread called "thalisio" or "thargilio", again the first one made with the cereals of the new crop. Until recently, this practice was still common in many parts of Crete.

Different kinds of bread were, and still are, baked according to the time of year and according to the feasts: Christmas breads ("Christopsoma"), "Lazaria" and "Lambrokouloures" at Easter, the "Fanouropites" on the feast day of Saint Phanourios and so on. Each region

has its own way of preparing and shaping these breads.

The decoration of the breads used to be of great importance and in some villages there are still old women called "xobliastres" who specialise in the decoration of breads, showing great experience and talent. In the village of Platanias in Chania, special bread rings are baked on the feast of the local saint, Ayios Dimitrios, and are known as Ayiodimitriatika or Dimitrokouloura.

Other breads of special interest are the holy ones: "artos" and "prosfora" (from "prosfero", to offer) with their special seal, breads for the celebration of baptisms, of engagements, of weddings, the bridegroom's bread, the best man's bread, the bread for the guests and so on. All these breads were particular to each region and the decoration, figurative and symbolic, was often a masterpiece.

Other breads, apart from the daily bread and the holy ones, are the "moustokouloura", the "paximadia" (rusks), the "stafidopsoma" (with raisins), the "koulouria" (rings) and many more.

Ancient customs of a definite folkloric interest have been handed down through the centuries: they refer to the planting of the cereals, the crops, the threshing, the milling and, finally, the making of the bread.

# THE CRETAN RUSK

M any try to emulate the Cretan rusk, but noone can succeed except the Cretans! It is not an understatement to describe the Cretan rusk today as "a product protected by geographical factors".

The rusk is a way of life on Crete! Barley rings (kritharokouloures), daci, wheat rusks, barley rusks, wheat and barley (migathero) rusks and "eftazymo" rusks are all names which call out to the distant or even recent past when the daily needs of life did not allow the housewife to make bread every day.

The double baking dried out any moisture in the bread, so that it became hard but tasty and would keep for weeks or even months.

These rusks can be easily dunked in some water to soften, although they can be eaten without being dampened. Cretans uncovered many ways of using rusks. The most famous is the barley kouloura with tomato and myzithra or the "koukouvajia" (owl), as it is known in some regions. These bread rusks are of various sizes and shapes. The round one is about 10-15 cm in diameter but there are smaller ones which are for individual portions.

The dried rusk is usually dark and made from wholemeal or barley flour. This tradition has never lost its roots on Crete. Every professional bakery today produces its own rusks and in the last few years, competition has been observed between the bakeries, as to which one produces the best rusks.

## SHAPE AND TEXTURE

Cretan rusks can be seen in a round shape (kouloura), a semi-circle, in other words like cutting a "turtle shell" in half (dacos).

Its texture is rough and uneven. On the upper surface, the fibres of the wheat and barley can be distinguished.

## TYPES OF CRETAN RUSKS

**Barley rusks**: In the traditional diet, this was the daily bread of the Cretans. These are made almost entirely from barley wholemeal flour.

Some bakers include a small amount of wheat flour in order to achieve a more favourable taste. These rusks are of a dark, usually brown colour. The barley fibres can be seen on the top surface of the rusk. It has a rather sour taste due to the leaven (prozymi) which is used in its making.

**Wheat rusks**: These are the official rusk of Crete. They are made from wheat, usually wholemeal flour. This type of rusk is not so dark; it is rather golden brown and has a less uneven texture. It is made for kouloures and "dacos", like the barley rusk. This rusk has a slightly sour taste.

## Wheat and barley rusks

This is another typical Cretan rusk which is extremely tasty and is made from a variety of flours (usually 50% barley and 50% wheat). It looks very much like the wheat rusk but it is a little darker. Its taste is rather sour.

## Wheat, barley and oats rusks

This type of rusk is not at all common. It can usually only be found in certain villages. It is made with varying amounts of wheat, barley and oat flour.

The rusk is slightly sour in taste but quite delicious.

## "Eftazymo" (chick-pea) rusks

These rusks are the official kinds of bread consumed on 15th August. They are usually made with sieved flour. The rusks are white in colour. They are not made with the normal leaven but with the speedy fermentation of the fungi contained in chick peas. "Eftazymo" rusks have a sweet and spicy taste, as they are covered in black sesame seeds. "Eftazymo" rusks are also sold in very small shapes.

**Rye rusks:** These are made with wholemeal rye flour. They are not very hard and there is a variety of shapes in which they are sold.

*A traditional "christopsomo"*

## The leaven

You need 1 cup wheat flour, a little salt and 1 cup warm water.

Make a hole in the middle of the flour, add the salt and the water and knead a very soft dough, actually a thick batter. Let the dough ferment in a warm place for 4 days. Then place it in a bowl (preferably earthenware), cover with a little olive oil and keep it in the refrigerator until you need it.

When you want to make bread, you take the sour dough out of the refrigerator, leave it at room temperature for 3-4 hours and then add more warm water and flour to make a thick batter again. Cover with a clean cloth and let it ferment again.

In the following recipes, beer yeast or dry yeast is used but sour dough can be used instead.

## The preparation of bread

It is the same for all kinds of bread.
Either yeast or sour dough can be used. In both cases prepare the leaven the evening before. One fourth of the flour is normally used for the leaven. Add an equal amount of warm water to the flour and make a thick batter.

The next day place the remaining flour in a large basin, make a hole in the middle and add all the ingredients there, either solid or liquid. Mix the flour, little by little with the other ingredients until very well combined and knead a malleable dough that does not stick to the hands. (At this point you can save a piece of dough for the next preparation of bread). Cover the dough with a clean cloth and leave it to rise in a warm place until doubled in bulk, in 2-3 hours.

Shape the bread, either oblong or round, place in oiled pans and let them rise again until almost doubled in bulk.

Bake in preheated oven until golden brown, for less than an hour.

*Right: A child is taking the christopsomo to the village oven in Anogia*

# The Christmas bread ("Christopsomo")

This used to be the main feature of the Christmas meal, in the countryside on Crete. Beautifully decorated and golden, it occupied the centre of the table. Its preparation was -and still is- something of a ritual: first the leaven, then the lighting of the fire, the kneading, the shaping... especially the shaping! In most parts of the island it had a large cross in its centre, which, if looked at side-ways, shows the letter X, the first letter of the Greek word for Christ. In other regions, the cross stood above the branches of a tree, also made of dough, on top of the Christmas bread. In different parts of the island it was more or less decorated with partridges, flowers and so on. Only the head of the family was allowed to cut this bread: holding the knife like a priest of ancient times, he made the sign of the cross, wished all those present (everyone was standing) a Happy Christmas and then cut the bread.

# "Christopsomo"

2 kilos flour
100 grams yeast
or 4 teaspoons dry yeast
3 cups sugar
1 teaspoon cinnamon powder
1 teaspoon ground mastic
1/2 cup olive oil
1/2 cup orange juice
2-3 cups water or "alousia"
(water boiled with ashes)
1/2 cup raki or cognac

Prepare the leaven the evening before: dilute the yeast in 1 cup water and add flour until you have a thick batter. (If you use dry yeast you don't have to do that).

The following morning, add the rest of the ingredients and knead soft dough.

Leave it in a warm place to rise until doubled in bulk and then divide into 2 balls saving a little dough for the decorative cross. Shape each ball into a round loaf and place in an oiled baking pan.

With the dough you saved roll out a thin rope and put it on the "christopsomo" in the shape of the cross.

Do the same with the other "christopsomo".

Let them rise again until doubled in bulk, then dab with beaten egg, place a walnut in the centre and bake in moderate preheated oven until golden brown.

# Country bread "Choriatiko"

2 kilos wholemeal flour
100 grams yeast or leaven
1 tbsp salt, or to taste
5-6 tbsps olive oil
4-5 cups water

Prepare the leaven the evening before: dilute the yeast in 1 cup water and add flour until you have a thick batter.

The next morning, add the remaining ingredients and knead a soft, elastic dough that doesn't stick to the hands.

Cover the dough with a clean cloth and leave in a warm place for about 2 hours to rise until doubled in bulk.

Shape oblong or round loaves, rub with a little olive oil and, with a sharp knife, slash 2 parallel lines across the top of the loaves.

Place the loaves in oiled baking pans, cover with a clean cloth, leave in a warm place to rise for 1-2 hours and bake in moderate oven for about 50 minutes until golden brown and sound hollow when taken out of the pan and tapped.

# Cretan Bread

2 kilos wheat flour
(or 50% wheat, 50% barley flour)
100 grams yeast
the juice of 2 cinnamon sticks
boiled in 2 cups water
1 tbsp salt
2 cups water or "alousia"
(prepare it by boiling 2 tbsps ashes in 2 cups water and sieving it afterwards)

1 teaspoon ground mastic and 1 teaspoon ground "machlepi" (both are strong sweet smelling spices)
sesame seeds

Prepare the leaven the evening before: dilute the yeast in 1 cup water and add flour until you have a thick batter. The next morning put the flour mixed with the spices in a large bowl, make a hole in the center and add the liquid ingredients there. Combine the flour with the liquids gradually until you have a soft and elastic dough. You might need to add some water or "alousia".

Leave the dough to rise in a warm place until doubled in bulk and then fashion long and narrow loaves, roll them in sesame seeds which have been sprinkled with a little sugared water, score the slices with a knife (but don't cut through) and put aside to rise once more. Then bake them in preheated oven for 45-50 minutes, until golden brown.

# Rusks

Make either "choriatiko" (country) bread or Cretan bread, or even "eftazymo" (chick-pea) bread and after you have shaped it, score the slices with a sharp knife, yet do not cut them through.

Bake the loaves for 40 minutes, take out of the oven and allow to cool off. Break off the slices and bake again at very low temperature (120°C) for 5-6 hours, until hard.

# Easter bread

2 kilos flour
150 grams yeast or leaven
3 cups sugar
8 eggs
1 cup butter, 1 cup olive oil
2 cups warm milk
1 teaspoon ground "machlepi"
1 teaspoon ground mastic
1 teaspoon grated orange rind

Prepare the leaven the evening before: dilute the yeast in the milk and add flour to make a thick batter. The next morning sift the remaining flour and sugar together in a large bowl. Make a well in the centre and add the leaven, the beaten eggs, mastic, machlepi, orange rind and olive oil. Combine the flour gradually with the other ingredients and knead. Heat butter to melt slightly and combine bit by bit with the dough until it is absorbed entirely and the dough is soft and silky.

Cover with a clean cloth and put in a warm place to rise until doubled in bulk. Then fashion the breads in various shapes, pressing down dyed eggs, if you want, and place in oiled baking pans, quite apart from each other. Cover and let rise for about 2 hours, until doubled in bulk. Dab with beaten egg and bake in preheated oven for about 30-40 minutes.

# "Eftazymo" (chick-pea) bread

5 kilos wheat flour
(or 50% wheat, 50% barley flour)
1 kilo chick peas
3 tbsps salt, or to desired taste
300 grams sugar
3 litres water
2 hot peppers
5 or 6 bay leaves
cinnamon, pepper, aniseed,
cumin (1 teaspoon of each)

Grind the chick peas and mix well with the finely chopped hot peppers, a little salt and a little warm water to make a batter. Cover the mixture and place it somewhere warm with constant temperature. It will take about 7 hours or overnight to rise and will have a little froth on top: this is called "kounenos".
Boil the remaining water with the bay leaves and let

cool off a little; add 1 litre warm water to the "kounenos", and a little flour to make a thick batter again.

Cover the batter and leave for about 2 hours to rise again. Then add the rest of the flour, the spices, the sugar and the water and knead a soft, elastic dough. Cover the dough, let it rise until doubled in bulk; then shape the "eftazyma" (several of them), either oblong or round.

Place in oiled baking or bread pans, quite apart from each other. Once these too rise, (in about 2 hours) brush the surface with sugared water and sprinkle with lots of sesame seeds.

Bake in a preheated oven for about 50 minutes.

*The beautifully decorated wedding bread is held high at the front of the wedding procession in Kritsa*

*The sanctification of the holy bread at a church on Crete*

# Wedding bread

5 kilos flour
(preferably wheat flour)
200 grams yeast or leaven
3 tbsps salt, 300 ml beer
1/2 cup olive oil
1 cup orange juice
1/2 kilo sugar
1 tbsp cinnamon powder
1 teaspoon grated nutmeg

Prepare the leaven the evening before: dilute the yeast in 1 litre warm water and add flour to make a thick batter. Cover and let stand overnight.

In the morning combine with the other ingredients and as much water as it takes to make a soft and elastic dough. Cover the dough with a clean cloth and let it rise in a warm place until doubled in bulk.

Then fashion the breads, round or oblong, roll them in sesame seeds that have been sprinkled with sugared water, place in oiled bread pans and let them rise again for about 2 hours. Finally, bake them in preheated oven for 45-50 minutes.

# Cretan holy bread

*The celebration bread (Artos) taken to the church as an offering and delivered to the faithful after mass on feast days.*

4 kilos flour *(preferably wheat flour)*
200 grams yeast, 1/2 cup wine
1/2 cup olive oil
1 kilo sugar, 1 tbsp salt
1/2 teaspoon ground mastic
1/2 teaspoon pepper
water, 3-4 bay leaves

The night before prepare the leaven as in the previous recipe. The next morning boil at least 3 litres water with the bay leaves and then cool it to becoming warm.

Sift the remaining flour, salt and sugar together in a large bowl. Make a well in the center and add the leaven, the mastic, the pepper, the wine, the olive oil and 2 litres water. Combine the flour gradually with the liquid ingredients and knead constantly adding more water, until you have a malleable dough. Cover and let rise for about 2 hours. Then divide into 5 parts and fashion the breads: shape two balls for each "artos", place one on top of the other and press them down with the special seal. Put in oiled bread pans, cover and let rise once again. Bake for about 40 minutes.

*Preparation of "manghiri"*

# PASTA

This was a very common food on Crete during the Turkish occupation.

The different ways of preparing pasta show an experience that has been handed down to us through the centuries.

Usually pasta was made shortly before being cooked, but many Cretan housewives found ways of drying it out but never in the sun, so as to store it and then it was cooked weeks, sometimes months, later.

Meals based on starch (or pastry) were easy and quick to prepare: especially for the cold winter evenings, when pasta was a light and wholesome meal mainly for the inhabitants of the countryside.

Among the better known Cretan kinds of pasta are the "manghiri" of Eastern Crete, "chylofta", lasagne, "skioufichta macarounia" and "chylobazina".

## "Manghiri"

1 cup water
1/2 kilo flour
(preferably wheat flour)
3 tbsps olive oil
1 teaspoon salt
1/2 cup olive oil for frying
1 cup grated "anthotyro"
(see the chapter on cheeses)

*This was a unique Cretan dish, usually served in the evening and in the countryside. Easy to prepare, it was very popular, especially during Lent, if it is served without the cheese.*

Prepare a dough with the water, the flour, the salt and the olive oil.
Let it stand for about an hour and then divide into 3-4 portions and roll out sheets 1/2 cm thick.
First cut each sheet into strips 1 cm wide and then into square pieces. Dredge

*Preparation of the traditional Cretan macaroni (skioufichta)*

them with flour so they will not stick and boil half of them in 2 litres salted water. Brown the other half in the oil and then empty them, together with the oil, in the pot with the boiled ones: stir and serve hot, sprinkled with grated "anthotyro" cheese.

# "Makaronia skioufichta"

1/2 kilo wheat flour
1 cup water
2 tbsps lemon juice
1 teaspoon salt
 6 tbsps olive oil
1 cup grated "anthotyro"
(see the chapter on cheeses)

Make a dough with the flour, the water, the salt, 3 tbsps olive oil and the lemon juice.
Let it stand for an hour and then fashion the pasta: shape a string of pasta the width of a finger and cut off pieces of about 3 cms long with your 2 fingers; press the fingers hard into the dough and rubbing them against the table, separate with skilful movements so as to shape short and thick macaroni (hollow in the middle).
Spread the macaroni on some flour to dry for an hour or so.
Then boil them in water with 3 tbsps olive oil for half an hour.
Take them out of the pot and on to a dish and serve hot with grated "anthotyro" cheese on top.

*Cretan women are cutting the pastry for the preparation of chylofta*

# "Chylos" or "Chylofta"

*A very common pasta dish, easy to prepare and therefore often made in winter when the family returned home exhausted from the fields at sunset, having harvested olives all day long. In some places this dish was known simply as "chylos", as in the Lent saying: "Forty days, forty chyloudies", that is, during the forty days of Lent one ate "chylos" forty times.*

*Often, to avoid having to prepare the dough every time, the "chylofta" were dried and stored and could thus be cooked at a moment's notice just like today's pasta.*

### Ingredients:
1 cup water
1/2 kilo flour
(preferably wheat flour)
1 teaspoon salt
6 tbsps olive oil
1 cup grated "kefalotyri"
or "anthotyro"
*(see the chapter on cheeses)*

Prepare the dough with the wheat flour, 3 tbsps olive oil, the water and salt: the result must be on the hard side. Roll out the dough and first cut out long strips and then long narrow pieces just like in the picture.

Boil in water with a little salt and 3 tbsps olive oil for about 20 minutes and serve with grated cheese.

Instead of grated cheese, you can mix some "myzithra" or "galomyzithra" with a little liquid from the "chylos" and at the end pour this over the dish so as to obtain a kind of soup.

# "Chylofta" with milk

Prepare the "chylofta" as in the above recipe but instead of using water for the boiling, use milk. Take care it doesn't boil over. You can also add sugar and less salt, if you want it sweet.

To be served as a soup: a thin crust forms on the top and many housewives sprinkle this crust with cinnamon powder.

# "Chylofta"
# with honey

*A special dish for women who have just given birth. It was believed to give the mother strength and that it was good for her milk.*

Boil the "chylofta" as above, in water. Use some of this water to dilute some honey, pour this over the "chylofta" and sprinkle with a little cinnamon powder.

*The ready-made pasta found nowadays can be cooked in the same ways as the hand-made pasta.*
*However, the most common way of cooking pasta in the last few decades is according to the wedding recipe: the famous Cretan macaroni boiled in meat broth, ideally goat, which is usually served on grand occasions with the macaroni.*

# THE HANDMILL ("CHIROMYLOS")

**E**very house had a stone hand-worked mill on Crete. Used for the preparation of many meals, it was an indispensable tool in every household in the countryside.

Whenever she ran out of bread, the Cretan housewife could quickly grind some wheat without having to go to the flour-mill. In this way she could also bake the famous pie called "chiromylopita".

The handmill is made of two large round chiselled stones, the "male" stone and the "female" stone.

The heavier bottom stone has a diameter of about half a meter and remains still when the handmill is in use. The stone is chiselled with care to form a cavity in the middle and its sides are 10 to 20 cm high, according to the stone.

Somewhere along the side there is a spout to let the ground cereal out. In the middle, a good sturdy "catch" (usually wooden, sometimes metal) holds the top stone in place.

The top stone is slighter and in its middle has a big enough hole for the "catch" around which it turns. It has a wooden handle on its side to make it turn.

Below you will find recipes which usually require the use of the handmill, but since this is not such a common tool you can buy roughly ground wheat in the market, or you can use an electric grinder.

# "Xinochondros"

*This is one of the most common foods of Crete. It is made of ground wheat and sour milk and can be eaten either fresh or after it has dried in the sun (in some villages in Amari and in Ayios Vassilios in Rethymnon they prefer drying it in the shade).*
*This isn't such an easy affair because cats love eating the "xinochondros" so often it is placed on a plank hung in mid-air, where the cats can't reach it.*

The **ingredients**:
3 litres fresh milk
(sheep's or goat's milk)
1 kilo wheat
3 teaspoons salt

Leave the milk out of the refrigerator for three days to go sour.
Grind the wheat, but roughly, not to the point of flour. In the old days the handmill was used for this operation.
Boil the milk, add salt and the wheat and stir till it is cooked and thickens. Once it cools a little, take the mixture out with a spoon and spread it on a floured tin or on clean kitchen towels.
Place the tin or the towels out in the sun to dry it, turning the pieces around every day. Store in clean cotton sacks.

# Goat soup with "Xinochondros"

1 kilo goat meat
1 cup "xinochondros"
salt, pepper

Wash and cut meat into portions. Place it in a pot with salted water to more than cover it and turn on the heat. Remove the froth as it starts boiling then let it boil until tender, about an hour and a half.
Take the meat out of the pot, strain the broth and add 2 more cups water to make the soup.
When it comes back to the boil, add the "xinochondros" and simmer till cooked, 10-15 minutes.

# Green beans with "xinochondros"

1 kilo green beans
1/2 cup olive oil
1 finely chopped onion
1/2 kilo finely chopped tomatoes
salt, pepper
1/2 cup "xinochondros"

Clean the beans by cutting off the tips and removing the fibres from the long sides. Rinse them.
Heat olive oil in a pot and add the onion and the beans. Sauté them for 10 minutes and stir in tomatoes, salt, pepper and 2 cups water or enough to cover them; (1-2 quartered potatoes can also be added).

Simmer until almost cooked and water absorbed, about an hour.
Add "xinochondros", stir and let it cook a further 15 minutes, shaking the pot occasionally.

# "Chondros"

*It is wheat that has been ground in the handmill. It was very widely used in Cretan cooking, and is especially good with snails. Equally good were the "dolmathes" stuffed with "chondros".*

*The main difference between "chondros" and "xinochondros" is that one is just wheat while the other, as we said before, is prepared with sour milk.*

*Often "chondros" was used instead of rice (as in "dolmathes"), either in mountainous regions where no rice was produced, or else because there was no rice to be found in the local market.*

# "Chondros" with leeks in tomato sauce

    1 kilo leeks
    1/2 cup olive oil
    1/2 kilo grated tomatoes
    2 cups "chondros"
    salt
    pepper

Clean the leeks, slice them up and brown in a pot with the olive oil.

Add the tomatoes and 1 cup water and simmer for about 20 minutes.

Pour 6 cups water in the pot and, when it comes to the boil, stir in the "chondros", salt and pepper.

Simmer until cooked, for about half an hour, but towards the end you have to stir often to prevent it from sticking to the bottom of the pot.

# Pork meat with "chondros"

    1 kilo pork meat
    1 finely chopped onion
    5-6 tbsps olive oil
    juice of 1 lemon
    3 tbsps vinegar
    2 cups "chondros"
    salt, pepper

Wash and cut meat into cubes.

Heat olive oil in a pot and sauté the onion and the pork turning it on all sides to brown evenly.

When the pork is nicely browned, pour in the lemon juice and the vinegar, along with 1-2 cups hot water.

Simmer for half an hour until almost tender and add 5 more cups of water.

Bring to the boil and stir in the "chondros", salt and pepper and simmer till cooked, stirring often to prevent it from sticking to the bottom of the pot.

*Right: "Chondros" with leeks in tomato sauce*

# CRETAN CHEESES

Cheese is one of the favourite foods of the Cretans, which is in stark comparison to their attitude to milk after childhood. The cheeses produced on the island are of a very high quality and are made from the milk of only goats and sheep. Cow milk is never used for cheese. Cretan cheese was well renowned even in ancient times as this was an exported product. The Cretan goat is kept according to the traditional methods whereby the animals range freely on the greens and herbs which grow in abundance in the animal farming areas of the island. There are no organised companies which specifically breed these animals for their milk on the island of Crete! Up until the 1960s, one particular cheese was produced, with a low fat content, a firm texture and a strong taste. (In the old days, the Cretans ate cheese which contained only a small amount of fat, in other words, a healthy cheese!)

## CRETAN "KEFALOTYRI"

This has been produced on Crete for many centuries as well as in many other Greek areas. It is made from only goat and sheep milk. It has a salty and rather spicy taste. It needs to mature for three months before it can be eaten. As a hard cheese it can be used either as a table cheese or for grating over pasta dishes.

# THE CHEESE OF MOUNT DICTE

The low fat cheese is still made in the area around the mountain of Dicte, in the mountainous areas of Pediada, in the Lassithi Plateau and the mountainous areas of Merabello, but it is extremely difficult to find on the market.

It is a hard, salted cheese with a strong taste.

It is made from milk from which the major fat content has already been removed. When it dries and loses its moisture, it can be kept in a jar of olive oil.

In general it can be said that this cheese belongs to the famous Cretan family of cheeses known as "kefalotiri", yet it is a traditional cheese which retains its own individual identity.

## "GRAVIERA" OF CRETE
### (A product of appellation of origin)

This is an especially delicious cheese which is slightly salted. It is made with sheep milk and is put on the market after it has matured.

Cretan Graviera is the most well known of the Greek cheeses. There is a rubber-like finish to the cheese and its surface can vary.

## "MALAKA"

Soft cheese, usually cut up into wedges. It is the same cheese as Graviera but it is used before it has matured, with all its moisture. It is especially used in the Chania area. Pies are made with this cheese, including some of the local specialities.

## "TYROZOULI"

This is a hard cheese with an exceptional taste and is produced in the area around Psiloritis and some other areas. Rennet is not used in its making but vinegar. Once it has dried, it is kept in a container of olive oil. A few decades ago, Sfakian "tirozouli" was the most famous one but nowadays, it is very difficult to find it anywhere.

## HARD ANTHOTYROS

This is an exceptional Cretan cheese. It is basically myzithra which has dried out and matured. It is a compact cheese with a strong taste, somewhat salty but on the other hand, full of aroma.

It is readily consumed on Crete. It is often grated to sprinkle on spaghetti or served as a good table cheese.

## "MYZITHRA" or SOFT "ANTHOTYROS"

This cheese is known as myzithra in eastern Crete and anthotyros in Chania, western Crete. It is made from what is left from the production of the other cheeses, so there is about 10-20% milk. When the myzithra takes form in the bottom of the pot, it is removed and placed in special baskets to strain so as to form their shape. As a soft cheese, there is a high level of moisture, a small fat content (16%) and a wonderful taste. It is used as a starter and a table cheese. This is the cheese that is used to make the well known Cretan kallitsounia and can also act as a lovely dessert with honey or grape-juice syrup, either uncooked or fried.

## "FETA"

This is not a traditional cheese of Crete as it does not seem to have been produced on the island in the old times. It is a soft white cheese, kept in brine and probably the most internationally famous cheese from Greece.

It has been produced in cheese dairies in central Crete since the sixties. It is used in traditional cooking and is an essential ingredient of the delicious "choriatiki" salad.

## SOUR MYZITHRA "XINOMYZITHRA"

### A product of appellation of origin

This is also a soft cheese. It is made in the same way as the normal myzithra but it is allowed to stand so that it matures and gains a rather acidic taste. It has a heavy flavour. Many pies are made on Crete with this particular cheese.

## "XYGALA"

This is a soft cheese. It is made from the milk which thickens without the use of rennet. It stands for 5-6 or even more days and then is strained. By then, it has attained a sour taste. It is used as a starter.

## YOGHURT

Ask for it when on Crete. It is delicious, with an exceptional taste due to the milk it is made with. It is used in the local cuisine (both in cooking and uncooked in dips) and is commonly served as a dessert with honey, fruit or nuts.

## "GALOMYZITHRA" OF CHANIA

### A product of appellation of origin

It is also known as "pichtogalo" (thick milk). Around Psiloritis, it is known as "athogalo".

It is a soft cheese, consumed after it has matured, with an almost cream-like consistency and made from goat milk. This is not only a delicious but also refreshing cheese which is usually served as a starter.

## "STAKA"

If you can find it on Crete, then try it! It is made during the process of making butter from the milk cream.

The milk cream ("tsipa") is heated with a little flour and immediately the butter is separated.

After the butter has been removed, a yellowish thick cream remains. That is "staka" which, if added to any dish, gives a very individual taste.

# "KALLITSOUNIA" AND "MYZITHROPITES"

**A**ll food (main dish or sweet) based on "myzithra" (either salted, sour or unsalted) is very popular on Crete.

"Kallitsounia", considered more as a dessert, were formerly part of every feast. The Easter meal was incomplete without them and, in most parts of the island, they were made on Holy Thursday morning, right after Mass. These "kallitsounia" were usually square and large and were baked in a wood lit oven which gave them a very special taste. During Carnival too, there were a lot of "kallitsounia" everywhere on the island, though "myzithropites", which were fried, were more common.

There is a great variety of both. The wonderful creativity of Cretan housewives found many ways of preparing these cheese pies: they differ not only in the preparation itself and in the cooking, but in the shape of the final product. "Kallitsounia" are usually round with a sort of a crown and are called "lychnarakia" (oil lamps) because of their shape; they can also be square, or triangular.

Myzithropites" on the other hand are usually semicircular, whether large or small. Aesthetics played as important a role as the taste and, thanks to the imagination of

Cretan women, the result in Cretan cheese pies is as pretty as it is savoury.

There is no one single way of preparing cheese pies on Crete: in Sitia, for example, they make "anevata kallitsounia", in character with the gentle disposition of the inhabitants; in Ierapetra and Merabello they make "nerates myzithropites" and in central Crete, "agnopites"; in Anoyia and the mountainous region of Mylopotamon the "myzithropites" are known as "sarikopites" from the "sariki" -the traditional head-dress Cretan men used to wear.

The "sfakianopites" from Sfakia are cooked in the frying pan with hardly any oil and the ones in Chania have no sugar.

# Cheese pastries with yeast from Sitia

For the **dough**:
2 kilos flour
1 cup olive oil
4 eggs
1 cup sugar
120 grams yeast
(leaven was used of old)
2-3 cups milk
For the **filling**:
2 kilos fresh unsalted myzithra
2 egg yolks
1/2 cup sugar
4 tbsps honey
1 tbsp cinnamon powder

Prepare the dough: the evening before, dissolve the yeast in 2 cups warm milk, add 2-3 cups flour to make a thick batter and let the leaven rise.

The next morning put the oil in another large bowl and amalgamate it with the sugar.

Add the remaining milk, the beaten eggs and the leaven. Combine gradually with the rest of the flour until you have a soft, elastic dough.

Let it rise for 1-2 hours until you get the filling ready by combining myzithra, yolks, sugar, honey and cinnamon.

Take pieces of dough the size of a walnut and roll each one into a 12 cm circle. Place 1 teaspoon of the filling on each circle.

Since the "anevata kallitsounia" are usually square, fold the two opposite sides in towards the centre each time.

Put the cheese pastries on baking sheet and leave aside for 1-2 hours to rise.

Brush them with a mixture of egg beaten with a few drops of lemon, sprinkle some sesame seeds over them and bake for about 20 minutes, until slightly golden.

# Easter "kallitsounia" (cheese pastries)

For the **dough**: 1 cup olive oil
1 cup milk, 1/2 cup sugar
1 teaspoon baking powder
diluted in 3 tbsps lemon juice
about 1 kilo flour
For the **filling**:
1,5 kilos "myzithra"
1 or 2 eggs

10 tbsps sugar
1 tbsp cinnamon powder
1 tbsp finely chopped mint
(optional)

Prepare the dough with the above ingredients, cover and leave aside to prepare the filling.
Combine the myzithra with the rest of the ingredients for the filling.
Take pieces of dough the size of a walnut and roll each one into a 10-12 cm circle. Place 1 teaspoon of the filling on each circle and shape them into small oil lamps by pinching the edges together (see the picture). Place in oiled baking tin or on baking sheet, dab with egg and sprinkle with cinnamon. Bake for about 20 minutes, till golden brown.

# "Tyropita" or cheese pie

1/2 kilo "filo" (paper-thin pastry that can be bought ready for use)
1/2 cup olive oil for the "filo"
2 cups milk
3 tbsps flour
3 tbsps olive oil
5 or 6 eggs
400 grams cheese
(preferably "kefalotyri")

Heat olive oil in a saucepan, add flour and stir for 5 minutes. Pour in milk and cook for another 5 minutes, stirring constantly until the mixture thickens. Turn off the heat and stir in beaten eggs and cheese.
Place 5 or 6 sheets of oiled "filo" sheets on the bottom of an oiled baking tin and spread the filling over it. Cover with the remaining oiled sheets of "filo" which you sprinkle with some water. Bake until golden brown.

# "Kallitsounia" with yeast from Rethymnon

For the **dough**: 2 cups milk
2 eggs
1 teaspoon salt

1 cup orange juice
1 kilo flour
2 teaspoons active dry yeast
For the **filling**:
1 kilo "myzithra"
200 grams feta cheese
1 egg
1-2˙ tbsps finely chopped mint
olive oil for frying

Dissolve the yeast in the warm milk, add the salt, the beaten eggs, the orange juice and the flour. Knead the dough which should be very soft.

Prepare the filling with both kinds of cheese, the egg and the mint.

Heat some oil in a pan. Have a cup of oil handy to oil your fingers every time you take a small ball of dough, so it won't stick. Press this ball down a little to place some filling in it, re-shaping the ball so as to close it. Flatten it out and fry it on both sides until golden brown. Repeat this operation until you use up all the dough and the filling.

You can serve these pies sprinkled with honey.

# Fried "kallitsounia" (small cheese pies) from Heraklion

For the **dough**:
1 kilo flour
2 eggs
4 tbsps olive oil
3 tbsps lemon juice
1 teaspoon baking soda
1/2 cup milk
1 cup water
1 teaspoon salt
For the **filling**:
1/2 kilo "xinomyzithra"
1/2 kilo "myzithra"
2 eggs
1/2 cup sugar
1 tbsp finely chopped mint
(optional)
1 tbsp cinnamon powder

Mix the oil with the lemon and the salt. Add the beaten eggs, the water and the milk; mix again. Work in the flour bit by

*This is the way the pastry is cut for the preparation of "kallitsounia"*

bit, mixed with the baking soda and knead until you get a malleable dough. Put the dough aside until you have prepared the filling, mixing all the ingredients until they are well blended.

Divide the dough into 5-6 parts, roll each one into a sheet 1/2 cm thick. Cut out circles 10-12 cms in diameter and place 1 teaspoon of the filling on each circle. Fold the "kallitsounia" like crescents pressing the sides with the help of a fork.

Fry in olive oil until golden brown on both sides and serve either with honey or sugar.

# "Sfakianopites" (small cheese pies from Sfakia)

*In Sfakia, cheese pies are prepared quite differently and this is due to the rather different kind of life in that region. Most inhabitants were stock-raisers until recently and so their food had to be dry enough to be carried up into the mountains. Sauces were out of the question in the White Mountains (Madara).*

*The frugal food, almost Doric in its simplicity, was particularly savoury and was based on the local dairy production.*

### Ingredients
### for 10 "sfakianopites":
1/2 kilo flour
3 tbsps olive oil
1 teaspoon salt
1 cup water
10 tbsps sour "myzithra"

Prepare a soft dough with the flour, the water, the oil and some salt.
Divide into 10 portions and roll each one into a circle 5-6 cm in diameter. Shape 10 small balls with the cheese and put one ball of cheese on each circle.
Pull the sides towards the centre so as to cover the cheese.
Press this ball down again with the pin to form new bigger circles, 15 cm in diameter.
Fry in a pan basted with hardly any oil, turning them upside down constantly so that they do not burn. Pour honey over each one before serving.

*The cheese pies from Sfakia are famous, both because of the excellent quality of their ingredients and because of the way they are prepared.*
*Professor Michael Defner travelled around Crete in 1919 and, having tried the cheese pies from Sfakia, wrote enthusiastically:*

*"O, my God, what relish! No king in the wide world has ever eaten a better pie. I must have had six or more and the others didn't lag behind!" (Defner, "A traveller's impressions of Western Crete", p. 147).*

# "Sarikopites"

1/2 kilo flour
1 cup water
3 tbsps olive oil
3 tbsps raki or lemon juice
1 teaspoon salt

**For the filling:**
1/2 kilo sour "myzithra"

Prepare a normal dough with the above ingredients.
Roll out the dough and cut it in strips 8 to 10 cms wide and 20 cms long. Spread the sour "myzithra" all along the strips, and fold them. Starting at one end, twist the ribbon in a spiral. The shape is similar to a "sariki" (the traditional head-dress of Cretan men which is why the pies are called "sarikopites").
Fry in olive oil until golden brown and serve with honey, grape-juice syrup or sugar.

# "Myzithroboureko" (Large "myzithra" pastry)

400 grams sour "myzithra"
250 grams "myzithra"
(fresh "anthotyros")
3 or 4 eggs
4 tbsps sugar
1 tbsp cinnamon powder

1/2 kilo ready made "filo"
(paper-thin pastry)

The **syrup**:
1 cup sugar
1 cup water
the juice of half a lemon

Combine the unsalted with the sour "myzithra", the eggs, the sugar and the cinnamon.

Place half the sheets of pastry ("filo") in a baking pan, oiling each sheet. Spread the cheese mixture on top and cover with the rest of the oiled "filo" sheets. Lightly cut the surface with a sharp knife to score the individual serving portions; sprinkle with a little water and bake in a moderate oven till golden brown.

Then take it out of the oven, let it cool and douse with the syrup you have prepared in the meantime.

Amalgamate the "myzithra" with the milk to become softer.

Divide the dough into portions, the size of a walnut. Open a small hole in the middle of each ball and fill with a tea-spoon of "myzithra". Pull the dough over to cover the "myzithra"; press down these balls and roll them out with the rolling pin to give them the size and shape of a saucer, 12 cms in diameter. Fry them in olive oil until golden brown and serve with honey, grape-juice syrup or sugar.

# "Agnopites"

For the **dough**:
1/2 kilo flour
1 cup water
3 tbsps olive oil
3 tbsps raki or lemon juice
1/2 teaspoon salt
For the **filling:**
1/2 kilo sour "myzithra"
3-4 tbsps milk

Prepare normal dough with the above ingredients.

# SWEETS

A peculiar sort of Cretan sweet made with flour, "plakoundas", was already famous in ancient Greece: the preparation of these "plakoundes" was rather special and had to do with the ingredients used, their shape and in general, the aesthetics of the time. To make them more attractive, the cakes were decorated in a geometric style and sometimes the dough was placed in specially designed moulds to acquire the desired form and then baked.

Other well-known sweets were called "**flepsia**", made with flour, honey and milk; "**itria**", made with boiled wheat or with sesame seeds and honey; and later on, a kind called "**pemmata**", with honey and "**sousamides**" reminiscent of today's "pastelli".

In ancient Crete, "**tiganies**" or "**tiganites**" were exactly the same as the ones that are so popular nowadays on the island, made then, as now, with flour and water and fried in very hot olive oil, served covered in honey or grape-juice syrup. The basic way of preparing sweets hasn't changed through the centuries, as is shown in different studies. Minoans used a lot of honey, sesame seeds and saffron. In classic years another famous Cretan sweetmeat was the "**glykinas**" which was made with sweet wine and oil, as we learn from Athenaeus in his book The Deipnosophists (XIV,53,645D).

This author also mentions the "**gastrin**" (The Deipnosophists XIV,57,647-648F), yet another Cretan sweet made with walnuts, almonds, sesame seeds, poppy seeds, pepper and honey:. This sweet was covered in ground sesame seeds, something like the "baklavas" we know nowadays.

In Venetian times, the most common sweet on Crete was "pastelli", the Byzantine "**pastillos**". But this "pastelli" was different from the ones that are prepared nowadays with honey and sesame seeds. Most certainly the Byzantines and the Cretans of the Middle Ages knew of "pastelli", a sweet made with must and flour, similar to "moustalevria" a very well known sweet in modern Crete ("moustos" is must and "alevri" is flour) which is dried out in the sun. In eastern Crete "moustalevria" is cut in rectangles or squares and these pieces are dried and are called "kiofteria". The word "pastelli" is not used on Crete to describe the famous sesame-and-honey cakes, as it rather implies figs dried in the sun.

The sesame cake famous from Byzantine times was called "**sisamaton**" or "**sisamitis**".

In modern Crete, honey and grape-juice syrup still continue to form the basis of all sweets and the other ingredients are all of local produce: the flour, the sesame seeds, the walnuts, the almonds, and many dairy products, like "myzithra" cheese. A number of old recipes have remained basically unchanged, though they have been adapted to new conditions and new needs.

The sweets based on "myzithra" have very old roots as well; unfortunately there aren't any sources so that we can compare how the housewives of the Middle Ages and the housewives of the 20th century used the same ingredients, quite possibly in the same quantities. What were known as "**tetiromeni plakoundes**" (Artemidoros in Oneirokr. 1,72) must have been something like the modern sweet Cretan "kallitsounia".

In the recipe notebooks of the 19th century that were consulted, the western influence is seen to have begun to be felt in the preparation of sweets; but this was only the case in town families that were well-off and who, in any case, knew the local recipes perfectly well. This was the time when the famous sweets called "glyka tou koutaliou" were at their height (literally, sweets of the spoon, referring to the fruit preserves served in very small quantities: pear, cherry, grape and quince are among the large variety of "glyka tou koutaliou"). There was a noticeable effort in the 19th century to use local fruit in the preparation of sweets.

# SWEETS IN THE CRETAN DIET

In folklore farming cuisine, sweets were rare! Sweets were made for special celebrations and each one had a particular sweet, such as "melamakarona" for Christmas and "kallitsounia" for Easter. There were more sweets in urban cooking as these were consumed much more regularly. Preserves and jams were the most common and could be found in most of the urban homes on Crete during the last few decades.

Sweets made from fruit were not to be seen on a farmer's table every day. On the other hand, honey and grape-juice syrup were never absent from any home. These were used as we use sugar today but in smaller amounts. Walnuts with honey, cheese with honey or grape-juice syrup always produced individual and interesting tastes. Further back in time, people always ensured that there were dried fruit in every home, especially figs and grapes.

Cretan grapes worked wonderfully with pomegranate pods and dried nuts, as a dish served to friends when they kept each other company during the long winter evenings.

The sweets in the traditional diet are natural, usually combining an aromatic flavour, but without the cholesterol and never over-eaten.

# CRETAN HONEY

There was a special kind of bee on Crete for thousands of years, the Apis melifica Adami, which is famous for the excellent quality of honey it produced. This was a small-bodied insect, bronze to golden in colour with yellow lines crossing its body. It was quite aggressive and resistant to diseases. Many writers in ancient times refer to it as, according to myth, the great god, Zeus, was nurtured on the honey of this bee. One of the most impressive finds from an archaeological dig on the island of Crete, is the discovery of the beautiful jewellery at Malia where there was a Minoan palace and this piece depicts two bees.

Linear B tablets, the most ancient written form of the Greek language, refer to honey with the same word that is still used today, "meli". In other words, the same word has been used for at least 3,500 years! The bee, "melissa", is the insect which produces the honey, "meli". In mythology it was Melissa, a Cretan woman, who nurtured the god, Zeus. She was the daughter of Melisseus, the king of Crete. These names prove the long-standing and befitting tradition of honey making on Crete.

Cretan honey is internationally renowned as one of the best in the world. It is aromatic and can vary in colour from golden yellow to a much darker shade with golden highlights.

It gets its flavour from the aromatic plants and herbs which grow in abundance on the island. A Cretan bee-keeper takes care

to move his hives to areas rich in flowers and aromatic plants, usually in mountainous areas, where the bees are free to roam and no chemicals are used on the plants.

Honey is full of natural goodness. Apart from its natural sweet substances, it contains many other important things (over 180) such as vitamins, aminoacids, minerals and enzymes.

This product is essential in a balanced diet. It also contains antioxidative agents, such as vitamin E, which help the human body to detoxify poisonous substances which enter from various sources, such as smoking and radiation.

The sugar level that it contains is of a different kind of glucose and so it permits even diabetics to use it in small amounts!

## HONEY IN THE TRADITIONAL DIET

Cheese or myzithra (fresh anthotyros) with honey was the most common dessert of the farming communities. Unbelievable flavours were achieved by making different kinds of pasties which were always accompanied with honey, such as myzithra pasties.

A special sweet was walnuts with honey and one which was offered to the bride and groom in the church during the wedding ceremony. It stood as a "sweet agreement" between the two parties and was also well known as being an aphrodisiac!

Honey was also put in the traditional teas and spread on bread for children. In some areas in western Crete, honey was even eaten with meat!

# Carrot spoon sweet

    1 kilo carrots
    1 kilo sugar
    3 cups water
    1 teaspoon vanilla extract
    the juice of 1 lemon

Clean and roughly grate the carrots. Cover them in water and bring to the boil till they are soft. Strain and keep 3 cups of the liquid. Return the carrots and this liquid to the pot, add the sugar and continue boiling until the syrup binds. Towards the end add the lemon juice, the vanilla extract and then remove from the fire. When cold, store in sterilized jars.

# Strawberry spoon sweet

    1 kilo sugar
    1/2 cup water
    1 kilo strawberries
    the juice of 2-3 lemons

Rinse the not-too ripe strawberries and put them to dry on a clean kitchen towel. Remove the stalks, place the fruit in an earthenware pot, pour over it the juice of the lemons and let stand for 8-10 hours. Boil the water and the sugar in a pot until a thick syrup is formed.

Add the strawberries and let them boil for 5 minutes. Let the mixture cool off and, with great care, remove the strawberries from the pot with a slotted spoon; place them on a plate.
Bring the syrup back to the boil and when it binds return the fruit to the pot. The preserve is ready; when cold, put in sterilized jars.

# Mandarine marmalade

    1/2 kilo mandarines
    1 kilo sugar
    1 cup water
    the juice of half a lemon

Wash and boil the mandarines until fork tender; then mash them. Add the water and the sugar and simmer until the syrup binds. At the end, add the lemon juice and remove the pan from the heat. When cold, store in sterilized jars.

# Orange spoon sweet

    1,5 kilos oranges, the kind
    with a thick peel
    1,5 kilos sugar
    3 cups water
    2 cinnamon sticks
    the juice of 1 lemon

*Orange spoon sweet*

Wash and drain the oranges and grate them slightly to release the oils. Rinse the oranges and boil them whole for about 20 minutes until they become soft. Drain them and cut each orange into 8 slices. Remove the hard parts with a pair of scissors.

Prepare the syrup with the water and the sugar and then plunge the orange pieces and the cinnamon sticks in this syrup, boiling constantly until the syrup binds again. Add the lemon juice and after a few minutes remove from the heat.

When cold, store in sterilized jars.

*One can also make an orange spoon sweet using only the orange rind; rub it clean, cut each orange rind into 6 pieces that you roll up and then tie to each other with a thread; boil them, bind them with the syrup and take away the thread.*

*In the same manner you can prepare preserves of bitter orange, citron, bergamot and other fruit, taking care to boil them first, then cut them and then leave them in cold water (which you have to change) for 1 or 2 days to get rid of the bitterness.*

# Fig spoon sweet

1 kilo fresh unripe green figs
1/2 kilo sugar
1 cup water
the juice of 1 lemon
1 teaspoon vanilla extract
or 5-6 cloves

Wash the figs and boil them for 5 minutes. Change the water and boil for another 5 minutes; then drain well.

Boil the water with the sugar for 5 minutes and add the figs.

Remove the pot from the fire and leave the figs in the syrup for 24 hours.

Then simmer till the syrup binds. Finally add the lemon juice and the vanilla extract or the cloves.

When cold, store in sterilized jars.

# Cherry
# spoon sweet

1 kilo cherries
1 kilo sugar
2 cups water
the juice of 1 lemon

Wash cherries and carefully take out the stones with a pit-remover.

Put the water, sugar and cherries in a pot and boil for ten minutes, removing the froth as it is boiling.

Let the mixture stand for 24 hours and then boil it again until it binds. Add the lemon juice 5 minutes before removing the pot from heat.

When cold, store in sterilized jars.

# Sour cherry
# spoon sweet

As above.

# Walnut
# spoon sweet

1 kilo small fresh unripe walnuts
1,5 kilos sugar, 3 cups water
1 stick of cinnamon
10 whole cloves, 2 lemons

Rub the walnuts clean and with the special knife open a hole through each one's center, from top to bottom. Cover them in water and boil them until fork tender, changing the water 2 or 3 times and replacing every time with fresh cold water. Drain and cover them in water once again, in a large bowl. For the next 2 days change the water regularly to get rid of the bitterness.

Put the water and the sugar in a pot and boil for 10 minutes. Drain the walnuts and add them to the syrup, bring to the boil; then turn off the heat and leave the nuts in the syrup for 24 hours.

The next day boil them again for ten minutes and let them stand once more for 24 hours.

The following day, bring to the boil and bind the walnuts with the syrup, adding the cinnamon, the cloves and the lemon juice just before the end.

# Quince
## spoon sweet

1 kilo quinces
1 kilo sugar, 3 cups water
2 sprigs of rose geranium
("amberosa")
the juice of 1 lemon

Peel the quinces, remove the seeds and the core and cut them into fine slices or roughly grate them. Prepare the syrup by boiling the sugar with the water for 10 minutes. Then add the quince pieces and boil constantly until they bind. A few minutes before removing the pot from the fire add the "amberosa" and the lemon juice.

# Grape spoon sweet

2 kilos grapes
(sultana kind)
1 kilo sugar
the juice of 2 lemons
1 cup water
vanilla extract or
2 sprigs of rose geranium
("amberosa", an aromatic plant)

Separate the grapes, remove the stems, wash and drain them.
Place the grapes in 3 layers in a pot, with sugar in between the layers. Add the lemon juice and let this stand for one day.
The next day, add 1 cup water and boil till the syrup binds.
Finally add the vanilla or the "amberosa". When cold, store in sterilized jars.

# New Year's cake

*This is the cake essentially prepared for New Year's day.*
*It always has a coin (traditionally a golden one) hidden in it: when the head of the family cuts the cake, he gives a slice to each one and the coin brings luck for the whole new year to whoever finds it in his slice. Slices of the cake are also cut for Christ, for Saint Basil whose nameday is on the 1st of January, and for the household as a whole: if the coin is in one of these slices, the good luck is shared by all.*
*According to tradition, this custom began in the time of the Saint (Basil the Great is one of the Orthodox church's most important saints). The enemy, it is said, was about to attack the city where he lived; in the hope of avoiding the pillage that would follow, he persuaded all the inhabitants to turn in their gold and jewelry. But in the end the city was not captured and the problem remained: how to give each one back his wealth. So the Saint came up with*

*the idea of baking small breads and in each one, hiding a coin or a piece of jewelry. When the breads were handed out, the miracle happened: each one, in his bread, got back what was his!*

# Saint Basil's cake

  1 kilo flour
  3 cups sugar
  1,5 cups olive oil
  1/2 cup cognac
  8 to 10 eggs
  2 cups orange juice
  2 tbsps grated orange zest
  1 teaspoon baking soda
  1 tbsp baking powder

Beat the yokes with the sugar and work in the oil and the orange rind. Dissolve the soda in the orange juice and add this. Beat the whites of the eggs; add half the flour, half the cognac with the baking powder diluted in it and half the egg whites. When this has amalgamated, work in the second half of the in-gredients.
Empty the mixture into an oiled baking tin and bake in a preheated moderate oven for about an hour.

# "Synnefiasmeno" (the "clouded" cake)

  1/2 cup olive oil or butter
  1,5 cups sugar
  7 eggs, 1/2 cup milk
  2 teaspoons baking powder
  4 tbsps cognac
  1/2 kilo flour
  1 cup grated chocolate

Beat the oil or butter with the sugar until creamy and add the beaten yolks. Beat in the baking powder diluted in the cognac and alternate the milk with the flour beating well after each addition. Finally add the beaten whites and comibine care-fully. Separate the mixture in two: add the grated chocolate to one half.
Oil a baking tin and spread one spoonful of the mixture with chocolate, one of the other, alternatively. Bake in preheated oven for about 45 minutes.

# "Revani" Semolina and syrup cake

  1/2 kilo yoghurt
  1/2 kilo coarse semolina
  1 tbsp baking powder
  1/2 cup sugar
  1/2 teaspoon vanilla extract
  **Syrup:** 2 cups sugar
  2 cups water

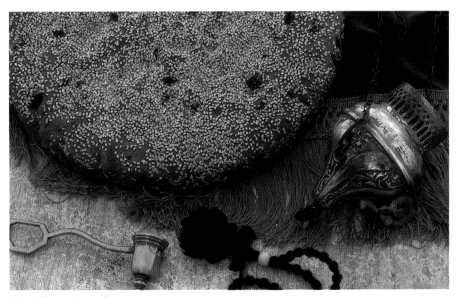

*Saint Phanourios' cake*

Dissolve the soda in the yoghurt. Beat in the sugar, the vanilla and gradually the semolina until creamy. Pour the mixture into an oiled baking pan and bake in a moderate oven for 30-35 minutes until golden brown. When it has cooled down, score the portions with a sharp knife, first vertically and then diagonally to form diamonds. Prepare the syrup by boiling the sugar with the water for 5 minutes and pour it over the "revani".

# Saint Phanourios' cake

*This is the cake made in honour of Aghios Phanourios on his nameday on the 27th of August: this Saint is particularly venerated on Crete, although some have doubted he ever existed and he's not mentioned in any of the Lives of the Saints. Many Cretans, on the other hand, believe that Aghios Phanourios can find lost objects, animals and even people if one invokes his help. Then, in an act of thanksgiving, a special cake ("phanouropita") is made and taken to church where it is given out to the faithful after Mass. On the 27th August, at dawn,*

*Cake with raisins*

one can see dozens of these cakes in many Cretan churches, especially those dedicated to the Saint: every housewife has seen to it that her cake is at least as savoury and as beautiful as the next one. Recipes of this cake are to be found in 19th century notebooks on cookery that we still have, proof that this custom is not a recent one.

**Ingredients:** 1 cup olive oil
1 cup sugar
1 cup orange juice
4 tbsps raki or cognac
1/2 cup walnuts
1/2 cup grated apple
or other fruit
1 tbsp ground cinnamon
and clove
1 tbsp baking powder
1 teaspoon baking soda
1/2 raisins
about 1/2 kilo flour

Begin beating the oil and the sugar until creamy, then add the cognac with the baking powder diluted in it, the baking soda dissolved in the orange juice, the cinnamon and clove, the raisins, the fruit and the wal-

nuts, beating all the while. Finally add the flour slowly until a thick batter forms. Pour it in an oiled baking tin, sprinkle with sesame seeds and bake for about one hour.

# Cake with raisins

1,5 cups olive oil
1 cup sugar
1 tbsp ground cinnamon
and clove
3 tbsps orange juice
3 tbsps cognac
2 teaspoons baking soda
2 teaspoons baking powder
2 cups raisins
1 cup roughly ground walnuts
about 1 kilo flour

In a large bowl, beat the olive oil with the sugar until creamy. Slowly add the cinnamon and clove, the soda dissolved in the orange juice and the baking powder dissolved in the cognac. When thoroughly mixed, add the flour to the liquids, bit by bit, then the raisins and the walnuts, beating all the time until all the ingredients are well blended. Pour the batter into an oiled baking pan and bake in a moderate oven for an hour or so.

# Apple cake

5 grated apples
1 roughly grated pear and
1 roughly grated quince
1/2 cup olive oil or butter
1 cup sugar
5 eggs
1 teaspoon baking soda
dissolved in the juice of 1
lemon
4 tbsps cognac
1 tbsp baking powder
1 tbsp ground cinnamon
and clove
1/2 kilo flour

First beat the butter or the oil
with the sugar, then add the
beaten yolks, the soda and
lemon juice, the cognac with
the baking powder dissolved
in it, the cinnamon and the
clove, beating continuously.
Slowly add the flour and the
fruit and mix thoroughly.
Finally beat the egg whites
stiff and gently combine with
the batter which should be
thick but liquid. Pour it in an
oiled baking tin and bake for
about an hour.
If desired, sprinkle with caster
sugar before serving.

# Cake with dried fruit and custard

1 cup olive oil or butter
5 eggs
2 tbsps ground cinnamon
and clove, 1 tbsp cocoa
1 teaspoon baking soda
1 tbsp baking powder
1/2 kilo flour
2 cups dried fruit
*(prunes, apricots, dates), which
have been doused with a little
cognac and 1/2 cherry syrup*
The **custard**: 2 tbsps corn flour
2 cups milk, 2 tbsps sugar
1 tbsp butter

Beat the butter with the yolks until creamy, then add the cinnamon and clove and slowly the flour sifted with the cocoa, the baking soda and the baking powder beating all the while. Finally mix in the fruit. Bake the cake in a moderate oven.
Prepare the **custard:** put the milk in a saucepan, start heating it and, when it is warm, dissolve the sugar and the corn flour in it, stirring constantly, until the mixture thickens; remove from the heat and stir in the butter.
Pour the custard over the cake and sprinkle with some grated coconut.

# Almond roll

150 grams "filo"
(ready-made paper-thin pastry)
300 grams almonds
100 grams sugar
150 grams candied fruit
3 eggs
The **syrup**: 1/2 cup sugar
1/2 cup water
juice of 1 lemon

Beat the yolks and combine with the sugar and the stiffy beaten egg whites. Add the almonds and the candied fruit.

Spread the "filo" sheets buttering or oiling each one and add the above mixture along the one side of the sheets. Wrap the filling with the "filo" forming a roll and bake until golden brown.
In the meantine prepare the syrup and pour it over the roll as soon as you take it out of the oven.

# Almond cake with custard

For the "**pandespani**"
(spongy cake):
1 cup butter or olive oil
2 cups sugar, 4 eggs
1/2 teaspoon vanilla extract
1 cup milk, 1 tbsp baking powder
2 cups flour
1 cup roughly ground almonds
For the **syrup**: 2 cups sugar
1 cup water
1 cup mandarine juice with 3
tbsps liqueur
For the **custard**: 6 cups milk
5 to 6 tbsps sugar
6 tbsps vanilla corn flour
1 tbsp butter, 2 eggs
1/2 cup bleached and roughly
ground almonds

Prepare the "**pandespani**": beat butter or olive oil with sugar until creamy and add yolks, vanilla extract, baking powder dissolved in the warm milk and flour, beating all the while until you have a thick batter. Gently combine the stiffy beaten whites and the almonds. Pour the batter into an oiled baking pan and bake for about 30-40 minutes. When the "pandespani" is cold, cut it horizontally into 2 parts.
Prepare the **syrup**: boil the sugar and the liquids for 5 minutes. Prepare the **custard**: put the milk in a saucepan, start heating it and, when it is warm, dissolve the sugar and the corn flour in it, stirring

constantly until the mixture thickens; remove from the fire and stir in the butter and the beaten eggs.

Place the 2 slices of "pandespani", one on top of the other, pouring half the syrup and spreading half the custard over each one in turn. Finally sprinkle the ground almonds over the cake.

# Walnut cake

5 eggs
1 cup sugar

4 tbsps cognac or raki
1 tbsp baking powder
1 teasp grated lemon rind
1 tbsp ground cinnamon
1 teaspoon ground clove
1 cup fine semolina
1 cup roughly ground walnuts
The **syrup**: 1 cup sugar
1 cup water
grated zest of 1 lemon
1 stick of cinnamon

Beat the whites of the eggs stiff and add the sugar. Then add the beaten yolks, the baking powder dissolved in the cognac, the grated zest, the ground clove and cinnamon and slowly the semolina and the walnuts, beating all the time.

Pour the batter into an oiled baking pan and bake in a moderate oven for about 50 minutes. After the cake has cooled down a bit, add the hot syrup which you prepare by boiling the above ingredients for 5 minutes.

# Phyllo pastry filled with custard "Galaktoboureko"

1/2 kilo ready made "phyllo"
1/2 cup unsalted butter for the "phyllo" sheets
For the **custard**: 7 cups milk
1/2 cup fine semolina
4 tbsps vanilla corn flour
1 teaspoon vanilla extract
1 cup sugar, 2 tbsps butter
4 eggs
For the **syrup**: 3 cups sugar
2 cups water, 1 cinnamon stick
the juice and the zest of 1 lemon

Prepare the **custard**: in a large saucepan start heating the milk. Immediately add the semolina, the corn flour and the sugar and stir constantly until mixture becomes thick and creamy. Remove from heat and add the beaten eggs, the vanilla extract and the butter, stirring constantly to combine them well.

Layer half the sheets of "phyllo" in a buttered baking tin, brushing each one with a little butter and spread the custard over them; now cover with the second half of the "phyllo" sheets brushing them, too, with butter.

With a sharp knife, lightly score the top sheets into diamonds or squares, sprinkle with a little water and bake in a moderate oven until golden brown. In the meantime simmer the ingredients for the syrup in a saucepan for 5-10 minutes and as soon as the 'galaktoboureko' is cooked, pour the syrup over it.

## "Gastrin"
## Nut-filled pastry

*This was a sweet prepared on Crete during ancient times. Athenaeus, the writer who gave us considerable information about the food and the nutrition of the ancient Greeks, recorded this "recipe", according to which, ancient Cretans made this sweet.*

For the **dough:** 1/2 kilo flour
1 teaspoon salt
4 tbsps olive oil
juice of 1 lemon, 1 cup water
100 grams roasted and ground sesame seeds
For the **filling**: 300 grams roughly ground hazel-nuts
300 grams roasted and coarsely ground almonds
300 grams coarsely ground walnuts
100 grams poppy seeds
1/2 teaspoon pepper
1/2 cup honey
For the **syrup**: 1 cup sugar
1/2 cup water
1/4 cup grape-juice syrup
1 cup honey
2 tbsps lemon juice

Prepare a soft and elastic dough with the above ingredients and leave it aside. Mix all the ingredients for the filling.
Divide the dough into 3 portions and roll out the

first sheet; place it in an oiled baking pan. Spread half the filling on the sheet and cover with the second sheet. Spread the remaining filling and top with the third sheet. Sprinkle with a little water and sesame seeds, score into diamonds and bake in moderate oven until golden brown.

In the meantime simmer the ingredients for the syrup in a saucepan for 5 minutes and as soon as the "gastrin" is cooked, pour the syrup over it.

# "Baklavas"
# (Nut-filled pastry)

1/2 kilo ready made "phyllo"
3/4 cup butter or olive oil
for the "phyllo"
For the **filling**: 2 cups roasted
and coarsely ground almonds
2 cups coarsely ground walnuts
2 teaspoons cinnamon powder
1 teaspoon clove powder
3 tbsps honey
For the **syrup**: 1,5 cup sugar
1 cup water, 4 tbsps honey
2 tbsps lemon juice

Mix the walnuts, the almonds, the honey and the ground clove and cinnamon. Melt the butter, butter a tin and spread 4 sheets of "phyllo", brushing each one with butter. Spread one third of the mixture and cover with 2 buttered sheets of the "phyllo". Repeat twice till all the ingredients are used up. On top place 6 buttered sheets of the "phyllo"; now score diamonds with a sharp knife, pour the rest of the butter over the "baklavas", sprinkle with a little water and bake in a moderate oven till golden brown. In the meantime, prepare the syrup and pour it, while warm, over the hot "baklavas".

# Roll of "baklavas"

3 cups ground walnuts
1/2 cup ground toasted bread
4 tbsps sugar
2 tbsps ground cinnamon and clove, 500 grams "phyllo" pastry
1/2 cup butter for the "phyllo"
The **syrup**: 3 cups sugar
2 cups water
2 tbsps lemon juice

Mix the walnuts, the bread crumbs, the sugar, the cinnamon and the clove.

On 2 buttered sheets of "phyllo" sprinkle some of the mixture; repeat the same procedure twice, covering the mixture every time with 1 buttered sheet of the thin pastry. Roll up the "phyllo" with the mixture in the middle and cut up the roll into 4-5 cm slices. Place them upside down in a buttered baking tin, pour the rest of the butter or oil over them and bake until lightly brown. In the meantime, prepare the syrup and pour it, while still warm, on the hot "baklavas".

# "Zournadakia"
# (Nut-filled rolls)

1/2 kilo coarsely ground walnuts
1/2 kilo roasted, roughly ground almonds

*Easter biscuits*

50 grams roasted, ground sesame seeds
1/2 cup sugar or honey
2 tbsps cinnamon powder
1 kilo paper-thin,
ready-made phyllo pastry
a cup and a half olive oil

The **syrup**:
4 cups sugar
3 cups water
the juice of 1 lemon

Mix the sugar or the honey with the ground almonds, walnuts, sesame seeds and cinnamon.
Cut every sheet of "phyllo" into 4 strips, oil each strip and sprinkle with a little from the above mixture (except for the edges).
Beginning at the bottom, roll the strips and place each roll in an oiled tin. Do the same with all the "phyllo" and all the filling. Pour very hot oil on all the rolls and bake in moderate oven until golden brown.
Prepare the syrup; put the rolls in it, bring to the boil and finally drain them.

# Easter biscuits

3 cups butter
2,5 cups sugar
1 cup milk, 3 egg yolks
1 teaspoon vanilla extract
1 teaspoon baking soda
3 tbsps cognac
the juice of 1 lemon
about 1,5 kilos flour

Beat the butter with the sugar until fluffy. Add the yolks, the vanilla extract, the milk, the soda diluted in the cognac and the lemon juice beating well after each addition. Slowly add the flour and knead a very soft and elastic dough
Take pieces of dough the size of a walnut and fashion the biscuits into various shapes; "S" curves, rings, coils, braids etc. Place on oiled baking tin or on baking sheet. Beat a whole egg, a yolk and a little lemon juice, brush the biscuits and bake for about 20 minutes until golden.

# Biscuits with jam

1 cup butter
1/2 cup sugar

3 eggs
1/2 teaspoon vanilla extract
1/2 cup roasted and roughly
ground almonds
about 2 cups flour
1 cup jam

Beat the butter with the sugar and add the yolks, the vanilla and the almonds. Beat in the flour little by little and knead very soft and elastic dough.
Roll out the dough to a thickness of 1 cm and cut out circles. Place them in a buttered tin, brush them with the beaten whites, sprinkle them with the almonds and bake for about 15 minutes. When the biscuits are baked and cold, stick them together with any jam you want.

# Small fried rings

1/2 cup olive-oil
1/2 cup sugar
3 eggs
1 teaspoon baking soda
1 teaspoon baking powder
1 tbsp clove and cinnamon
powder, 4 tbsps cognac
2-3 cups flour
olive oil for frying
caster sugar for sprinkling

Beat the oil with the butter. Add the yolks, one at a time and then the whites beaten stiff, the soda and the baking powder dissolved in the cognac, the clove and the cinnamon, beating well after each addition. Gradually stir in the flour and knead thoroughly into a very soft dough. Shape very small rings: take a little dough at a time, a little smaller than the size of a walnut and roll it into a thin rope, 8-10 cms long. Form a circle with it. Do the same with the rest of the dough.
Deep-fry the rings in olive oil. Place on kitchen roll to dry.
Sprinkle them with caster sugar and serve either hot or cold.

*Small butter rings*

# Small butter rings

1 cup butter, 1 cup sugar
2 yolks, half a cup milk
1 teaspoon grated orange zest
1 tbsp baking powder
4 cups flour

Beat the butter with the sugar very well. Add the rest of the ingredients, beating constantly, until very soft and malleable and then let the dough stand for about an hour.
Finally shape the rings: take a little dough at a time, the size of a small walnut and roll it into a thin rope, 10 cms long. Form a circle with it and place on baking sheet or in oiled baking pan far apart from each other. Brush them with beaten egg and bake in a moderate oven for 15-20 minutes.

# Small olive oil rings

1,5 cups olive oil
1 cup sugar, 1,5 cups orange juice
1/2 cup cognac
1 tbsp baking powder

*Small olive oil rings*

1 teaspoon baking soda
1,5 kilos flour (more or less)
2 cups sesame seeds

Beat the sugar with the olive oil and add the other ingredients beating constantly until they are thoroughly mixed and very soft and elastic dough is formed.
Shape the rings as above, pour a little liqueur on them, sprinkle with some sesame seeds and place on baking sheet or in oiled baking pan far apart from each other. Bake in a moderate oven for 15-20 minutes.

## Small olive oil and wine rings

1,5 cups olive oil
1,5 cups sugar
1,5 cups white wine
1,5 teaspoons baking powder
1,5 teaspoons baking soda
1 tbsp clove and cinnamon powder
1/2 cup orange juice
1,5 kilos flour
2 cups sesame seeds

Beat the sugar with the olive oil and continue with the baking powder dissolved in the wine, the soda dissolved in the orange juice, the clove and the cinnamon. Gradually add flour to the liquids and knead very soft and malleable dough.
Shape the rings as above, sprinkle them with sesame seeds and bake in moderate oven for 15-20 minutes.
Using the same recipe, you can make delicious rusks ("paximadakia").

## Small barley rings

1,5 cups olive oil
1,5 cups sugar
1/2 cup raki or cognac
1/2 cup orange juice
1 tbsp cinnamon and clove powder, 1 tbsp baking soda
more or less 1 kilo barley flour

Beat the sugar with the olive oil and add the other ingredients beating constantly until they are thoroughly mixed and very soft and elastic dough is formed.
Shape the rings as above; bake in moderate oven for 20 minutes or so.

## «Patoutha»

The **dough:** 2 cups olive oil
1 cup "alousia" or water
(*you can prepare alousia by boiling 1 tbsp wood ash in 1 cup water, then strain and discard the ash*)
1 cup orange juice
4 tbsps cognac
1 tbsp baking soda
more or less 1,5 kilos flour
The **filling:** 1 kilo roughly ground walnuts and almonds
1 cup honey and
1 cup sugar, 1 cup water
1 tbsp grated orange zest
4 tbsps olive oil
1/2 teaspoon grated nutmeg
1 tbsp ground clove and

cinnamon
4 tbsps ground toasted bread

Prepare the dough; in a large bowl, beat oil a little and add the other liquids and the soda dissolved in the cognac. Finally add flour, bit by bit and form soft, smooth dough.

Prepare the filling: In a saucepan heat water and add honey, olive oil and sugar; simmer for 2-3 minutes. Let it cool to

being just warm and mix with nuts, zest, nutmeg, clove and cinnamon and finally the bread.

Separate the dough into small balls the size of a mandarine. Roll out these balls into 12 cm circles and place 1 tbsp of the filling on one half of each. Fold over to form crescents and press the edges together. Place on baking sheet or on oiled baking pan and bake for about 20 minutes, until golden. When they have slightly cooled, sprinkle with caster sugar.

# Small almond or walnut rusks

3 cups olive oil
3 cups sugar
2 cups roasted and roughly ground almonds or walnuts
1 cup orange juice
1/2 cup cognac
1 teasp. grated orange zest

1 cup warm water
1 teaspoon baking soda
4 tbsps baking powder
2 teaspoons cinnamon
2,5 kilos flour (more or less)

Beat the oil in a large bowl and stir in the sugar, the nuts, the zest, the cinnamon, the water, the soda dilssolved in the orange juice, the baking powder diluted in the cognac and finally the flour. Knead thoroughly until you have soft, malleable dough and then shape small loaves. Cut the surface into slices (but not all the way down; the loaf has to remain whole) and bake for about half an hour. Now break away each slice and bake again in a temperature of 120o C until hard.

# Small raisin-filled patties

The **dough:** 2 cups olive oil
1 cup sugar, 1 cup orange juice
1/2 cup cognac or raki
1 tbsp grated orange zest
1 tbsp baking powder
1 teaspoon baking soda
1,5 kilos flour (more or less)
The **filling**: 1 kilo roughly ground raisins
2 cups roughly ground walnuts and almonds, 2 tbsps olive oil

1 teaspoon grated lemon rind
2 tbsps clove and cinnamon powder

Prepare the **dough**: beat together olive oil and sugar and add zest, baking powder dissolved in cognac and baking soda dissolved in orange juice, beating constantly. Gradually add flour to the liquids until you have soft and elastic dough. Mix the ingredients throroughly for the filling. Take pieces of dough the size of a walnut and in the middle open a well to put in a little filling. Roll the

dough in your hands so as to get the filling to spread inside and shape oblong "stafidota".

# Small raisin rusks

The ingredients and the preparation are exactly the same as for the above recipe. They only differ in the shape, which is as follows: break off the dough into several parts and roll out into rectangular sheets, 10-12 cms wide and 25-30 cms long. Spread some filling along the long side and fold carefully to shape loaves enclosing the filling. Place in oiled baking pan, cut the surface into slices (but not all

the way down: the loaf has to remain whole). Bake for about 25 minutes. When they cool down, break away each slice.

# Grape-must syrup ("Petimezi")

To make "petimezi" use fresh sweet grapes. Wash 10 kilos grapes and press them through a sieve with a bowl underneath to get their juice. Strain and put it in a pot discarding the pulp and seeds. There must be about 5 litres juice.

Tie 1 cup wood ash in a clean, white cotton cloth and submerge it into the must. Bring the must with the ash to the boil and simmer for 10-15 minutes removing the froth formed on the surface all along. Turn off the heat and discard the sac with the ash. Let the must stand overnight.

The next day transfer the must to another pot through 2 layers of fine cotton cloth, taking care not to upset the residue which you discard. Bring the must to the boil again and simmer over medium heat until it goes brown and turns to a thick syrup. (It should be reduced to 1/3 by then). When it cools down, store in jars.

*This grape-juice syrup is used, like honey, in the preparation of many sweets and pies.*

# Grape-must syrup biscuits

1 cup olive oil, 1 cup sugar
1 cup grape must (or syrup)
1/2 cup orange juice
1 teaspoon baking soda
4 tbsps cognac
2 teaspoons baking powder

# Dried figs with grape-must syrup

1/2 kilo dried figs
1 cup ground walnuts or almonds
1 teaspoon cinnamon powder
1 teapoon clove powder
1/4 cup grape-must syrup
1/4 cup ouzo or cognac

Wash the dried figs, pat dry and grind them. Combine with the other ingredients until a malleable paste is formed. (Add more ouzo or cognac if needed).
Break off the thick paste into portions the size of a small orange and press them into round or oval "sykopita-rides", 2-3 cms thick.
Sprinkle with sesame seeds and bake in a moderate oven for 6 minutes, until the grape-must syrup sets. Put them in layers in a jar with laurel leaves imbetween.

*Grape must jelly*

2 teaspoons clove and cinnamon powder
1 kilo flour (more or less)

Beat the oil with the sugar and then with the must, the soda dissolved in the orange juice, the baking powder dissolved in the cognac, the clove and cinnamon. Slowly combine the flour with the liquids and knead very soft dough. Shape the rings: take a little dough at a time, the size of a small mandarine and roll it into a thin rope, 12-15 cms long. Form a circle with it and place on baking sheet or in oiled baking pan, far apart from each other. Bake in a moderate oven for 15-20 minutes.

# Grape must jelly

6 cups boiled must *(see above, the preparation of petimezi)*
1 cup flour
1/2 cup roughly chopped walnuts
1 tbsp cinnamon powder
2 tbsps sesame seeds

The must needed for moustalevria must have been clarified, so follow the instructions for making petimezi until the step that you sieve the boiled must and dis-

card the residue. Now put the must in a pot, boil for 15 minutes and let it cool (It will now have been reduced to 5 cups. Dilute the flour in a little cold must and set aside.

In a large pot bring the remaining must to the boil and add the flour mixture stirring constantly as it boils, with a wooden spoon. Lower the heat and, always stirring, wait till the mixture thickens.

Remove the "moustalevria" from the heat and empty it on to several small plates or onto larger ones. Sprinkle with the walnuts, the cinnamon and the sesame seeds and let it cool. You can also add some walnuts in the jelly when you are stirring in the diluted flour.

# "Amigdalota" or almond confections

1 kilo blanched and roughly ground almonds
1 kilo caster sugar

*Small apple pastries*

8 egg whites
2 tbsps grated lemon zest

Mix almonds with sugar and zest and slowly add the stiffy beaten egg whites; knead until the paste is malleable. Shape the paste into balls or any other shapes and bake for about 15 minutes.

# Small apple pastries

For the **dough:** 2 cups olive oil
1/2 cup sugar, 2 eggs
2 teaspoons baking powder
4 tbsps cognac or raki
grated rind of 1 lemon
1/2 kilo flour
For the **filling:** 1 kilo yellow apples, 4 tbsps sugar
1 tbsp cinnamon and clove powder
4 tbsps raisins
4 tbsps roughly ground walnuts

Beat olive oil with sugar and add egg yolks, lemon rind, baking powder dissolved in cognac, beaten eggs and finally the flour, little by little. The dough should be soft and malleable.

Peel and grate the apples and mix with the rest of the ingredients for the filling. Break up the dough into small balls the size of a walnut. Roll out these balls into circles 12 cms in diameter and place 1 teaspoon of the filling on one half. Fold over to shape crescents and place on baking sheet or in oiled baking pan. Bake in moderate oven for about 20-25 minutes. When they have cooled down, sprinkle with caster sugar and cinnamon.

# Chocolate truffles with chestnuts

700 grams chestnuts
800 grams butter
1 cup caster sugar
2 cups roughly ground walnuts
250 grams confectionery chocolate
4 tbsps liqueur
250 grams chocolate truffle

Boil, peel and mash the chestnuts. Add the melted butter, the melted chocolate and the sugar. Stir while adding the liqueur and the walnuts; combine tho-

*"Kourabiethes" and "Melomakarona"*

roughly and let the mixture cool down. Then shape little balls with the mixture, roll them in the chocolate truffle and place each ball in a special little truffle paper case.

# Small almond cakes "Kourabiethes"

> 700 grams butter
> 300 grams olive-oil
> 1/2 cup caster sugar
> 3 yolks and 1 egg white
> 1 teaspoon baking soda
> 3 tbsps cognac
> 1 tbsp cinnamon powder
> **700 grams blanched and roughly ground almonds in their skins**
> about 1200 grams flour
> 1/2 kilo caster sugar

In a large bowl beat the butter and the oil with the sugar until fluffy. Stir in the beaten eggs, the soda diluted in the cognac, the cinnamon and the almonds. Gradually combine the flour with the mixture and knead thoroughly until the dough is malleable. Take pieces of dough the size

of a walnut and give them either a round or an oblong shape. Bake the "kourabiethes" for 15-20 minutes. When they are slightly cold, sift caster sugar over them until they are completely dusted.

# "Kourabiethes" with syrup

> 1 cup sugar, 1 cup water
> 1/2 kilo butter, 3 yolks
> 1 tbsp baking soda
> the juice of half a lemon
> flour (a kilo, more or less)
> **The syrup:** 3 cups sugar
> 3 cups water

Boil 1 cup of sugar in 1 glass of water for 5 minutes. When it is just warm, beat the butter till it goes pale and little by little add the syrup, the yolks, the baking soda dissolved in the lemon juice and the flour beating all the time. Knead until the dough is smooth and silky. Then shape the kourabiethes as above and bake them.

Prepare the syrup and when the "kourabiedes" have cooled to warm, carefully pour the syrup over them with a spoon.

# Small honey cakes "Melomakarona"

1,5 cups olive oil
1/2 cup caster sugar
1/2 cup orange and lemon juice
1 teaspoon grated orange rind
1 teaspoon clove and cinnamon powder
2 teaspoons baking soda
1/2 cup raki or cognac
1 teaspoon baking powder
1 kilo flour (more or less)
The **syrup**: 1 cup honey
1 cup sugar, 1 cup water
1 stick of cinnamon
ground walnuts and cinnamon powder

Beat the oil and the sugar together and then add the cinnamon and clove, the lemon rind, the soda diluted in the fruit juice, the baking powder diluted in the raki and finally the flour, little by little until you have soft dough that doesn't stick to the hands. Knead thoroughly and then take pieces of dough the size of a small egg and make them oblong. Place on baking sheet or in oiled baking pan, far apart, and bake in a moderate oven for about 20 minutes, until golden brown.

While they are cooling prepare the syrup. While the syrup is boiling over low heat, dip the "melomakarona" in for 1 minute to absorb syrup and to moisten. Take them out with a slotted spoon, put on to a plate and sprinkle with the mixture of the walnuts and the cinnamon.

# Christmas biscuits

1 kilo flour
1/2 kilo honey
2 cups sugar
1 cup roasted, coarsely ground almonds
1 cup candied fruit
grated rind of 3 oranges
1 tbsp cinnamon powder
1 teaspoon clove powder
1 tbsp baking powder
2 eggs
2 tbsps butter

Sift flour with sugar, cinnamon and clove, orange rind and baking powder. Make a well in the center and add the honey, the beaten eggs, the slightly melted butter and the almonds.

Gradually combine the flour with the liquids until the dough is soft and malleable.

Let it stand for half an hour and then divide into portions which you roll out into sheets, 1/2 cm thick. Cut out the biscuits in any shape you like. Bake for ten minutes in a moderate oven.

*Melomakarona without syrup*

# "Chalvas" Semolina and syrup pudding

1 cup olive oil
1/2 cup coarse semolina
1 cup fine semolina
1/2 cup roughly ground walnuts
1/2 cup pine kernels
1 tbsp clove and cinnamon powder
The **syrup**: 2,5 cups sugar
4,5 cups water
1/2 cup raisins
1 stick of cinnamon

Heat the oil in a saucepan with the peel of an orange; when the oil is hot enough, remove the orange peel and add the semolina, the cinnamon, the walnuts and the pine kernels, stirring constantly.

In another pot prepare the syrup and when the semolina is golden brown, carefully pour the syrup in the pot; stir vigorously for 5-6 minutes.

The "chalvas" can be served in a large mould or in several small ones.

# Baked "chalvas"

1/2 cup butter
1 cup sugar
1 cup yoghurt, 3 eggs
1,5 cups semolina
1 tbsp baking soda
2 tbsps cognac
1/2 cup roughly ground walnuts or almonds
1 tbsp cinnamon powder
The **syrup**: 2 cups sugar
2 cups water
1 stick of cinnamon

Beat together the butter, the sugar and the yoghurt. Add the beaten yolks, the semolina, the soda dissolved in the cognac, the cinnamon and the walnuts or the almonds, beating all the time. Beat the egg whites stiff and combine with the mixture.

Pour the mixture into a buttered baking tin and bake in a moderate oven. After you have taken the "chalvas" out of the oven, pour the hot syrup over it, which you have prepared in the meantime.

# Fritters "Xerotigana"

1 kilo flour
1/2 cup raki or lemon juice
1 tbsp olive oil

1 tbsp salt
as much water as needed
(about 2 cups)

For the **syrup:**
2 cups sugar
2 cups water
1 cinnamon stick
1 cup honey
3 tbsps lemon juice
cinnamon powder and ground
   nuts for the sprinkling

Knead rather smooth and elastic dough with the above ingredients.

Roll out the dough to long, almost paper-thin strips, 3 cm wide and 25 cm long. Heat the oil in a pan. Wrap one strip at a time around your fingers, first using two fingers, then three and then four; stick the edge and deep-fry. With the help of two forks, turn these rings upside down, taking care not to spoil the shape. When each fritter is nice and brown, take it out of the pan and place it on kitchen roll.

Prepare the syrup when all the fritters are ready. Boil the sugar in water, with the cinnamon, for 5 minutes and then add the honey and the lemon. Dip each fritter in the very hot syrup and when you take it out, place it on a dish and sprinkle with the nuts (or sesame seeds) and the cinnamon.

# Fritters "Avgokalamara"

5 eggs
5 tbsps olive oil
5 tbsps sugar
5 tbsps raki or lemon juice
1 cup milk

1 tbsp baking powder
1 kilo flour, more or less
The **syrup**: 1 cup sugar
1 cup water
1/2 cup honey
1 tbsp cinnamon
powder, ground
walnuts and sesame seeds

Beat the oil with the sugar and the raki or lemon juice, the milk and the baking powder dissolved in it, beating after each addition. Little by little mix in the flour and knead thoroughly until malleable dough is formed.

Roll out the dough to a thickness of half a centimetre and cut out squares of 10 by 10 cms which you wrap in the shape of cones with the help of two forks; these you deep-fry. Then place them on absorbing kitchen roll and prepare the syrup.

Finally, dip each "cone" or "avgokalamaro" in the boiling syrup, take out immediately with a slotted spoon and place on a plate. Sprinkle with walnuts or sesame seeds and cinnamon.

# Beignets or "Svingi"

1 cup water
1 cup flour
1/2 cup olive oil
6 eggs
1 teaspoon salt
2 teaspoons baking soda
olive oil for frying
For the **syrup**: 1 cup sugar
1/2 cup water
2-3 tbsps honey
2 cinnamon sticks
1 lemon rind, 3 tbsps cognac

In a pot put the water, the soda, the olive oil and the salt. Bring to the boil, add the flour and stir vigorously with a wooden spoon until the paste leaves the sides of the pan. Take from the heat and let it stand for a few minutes. Then beat each egg and mix with the paste, one at a time, stirring vigorously after each addition. Have a deep pan with ample oil ready and when very hot, take a teaspoon of the paste and drop into the pan one at a time, taking care to dip the spoon every time into cold water to keep the paste from sticking on to it. When the "svingi" are golden, take them out of the oil, place on a plate and sprinkle with caster sugar mixed with cinnamon.

You can also serve them doused with the syrup which you make with the above ingredients.

# Pancakes (Tiga-nites)

2-3 cups water
1 tbsp olive oil
1 tbsp lemon juice
1 teaspoon salt
1/2 kilo flour
honey or grape-must syrup
sesame seeds and ground walnuts

Sift the flour with salt in a bowl, open a well in the middle and put in the oil and the lemon juice.

Mix, add water and keep on stirring vigorously until you obtain a thick batter. Have a deep pan with oil ready and when it is very hot, take tbsps of batter and drop them in the oil, one at a time. When the pancakes are golden, place them on a plate, pour some honey or grape-must syrup and sprinkle sesame seeds and ground walnuts over them.

# "Loukoumia" Spongy fritters

1 cup olive oil
1 cup sugar
1 cup orange and lemon juice
3 tbsps cognac
1 teaspoon salt
1 teaspoon ground mastic
1 teaspoon cinnamon powder
2 teaspoons active dry yeast
1 kilo flour (more or less)
olive oil for frying
**Syrup**:
2,5 cups sugar
2 cups water
juice of 1 lemon

Dissolve the yeast in 3 tbsps warm water and add olive oil, sugar, orange juice, cognac, salt, mastic and cinnamon, stirring all the time. Gradually combine flour until the dough is soft and silky and let it stand for half an hour.

Take pieces of dough to form rope 3-4 cms thick and cut slices every 3 cms. Deep fry until golden brown and dip immediately into the syrup which you have prepared. Take them out with a slotted spoon and place on a plate.

# Dry measures

1 cup flour = 150 grams
1 cup semolina
   or caster sugar = 130 grams
1 cup sugar = 230 grams
1 cup rice = 230 grams
1 cup grated cheese = 100 grams
1 cup chopped almonds
   or walnuts = 100 grams

# Liquids

1 cup = 225 ml
1 cup = 16 tablespoons (tbsps)
1 tablespoon
   (tbsp) = 3 teaspoons
1 tablespoon = 15 ml
1 teaspoon (teasp.) = 5 ml